ANSWERS
IN ABUNDANCE

A Miraculous Adoption Journey
as Told from a Father's Heart

ELLIOTT J. ANDERSON

New York

Paperback ISBN: 978-1-60037-232-2
Hardcover ISBN: 978-1-60037-233-9

Published by:

MORGAN · JAMES
THE ENTREPRENEURIAL PUBLISHER™

Morgan James Publishing, LLC
1225 Franklin Ave. Ste 325
Garden City, NY 11530-1693
Toll Free 800-485-4943
www.MorganJamesPublishing.com

Cover & Interior Design by:

Paper Tower Inc
www.papertower.com

CONTENTS

IV. THE BIOLOGICAL SURPRISE

V. THE ADDITIONAL BLESSINGS

Acknowledgements
and Preface

This is not intended to be a self-help book on adoption. The road to adoption is so unique that no two adoption experiences could ever be the same. Nor is it a book on conception strategies. The fact that my wife and I conceived two biological girls after adopting identical twin boys is no guarantee that pattern will work for other couples. There is no statistical evidence that adoption leads to conception.

I wrote this book for four specific reasons. First, it was a therapeutic experience. As I typed the words into the computer keyboard throughout 2001, there were many times that I processed—for the first time—the events of the past decade, and fully understood their significance in my life. After the magazine, *Adoptive Families* published my article on what to do when an adoption placement fails, a fire for writing this story was ignited.

Second, I wrote this book because so many of my friends, family, and colleagues suggested it. So during Christmas break 2000, long before our daughters were born, I began the writing.

As I finished a few pages and passed them around to friends for critique, I was greatly encouraged by their positive remarks.

I want in particular to say thanks to my sister, Karin, who offered valuable initial feedback and crucial ending editing. Thanks to my brother-in-law, Brock, for his tech, graphics, and layout skills, and the opportunity for me to be an older brother these last 20 years! Thanks to Linda Cain for her suggestions and adjustments in the initial draft; thanks to Cathy Peterson for clarity and precision in the second draft; thanks to my brother, Warren, for his analysis of the book-at-large; thanks to Tim and Laura Perry for believing in this vision and coordinating God's hands and feet to Morgan James Publishing; and thanks to Simon Anderson, my father and the primary editor for every draft; and to both my parents for being the life encouragers, motivators, and financial supporters of this project and all other projects in the lives of their children!

Third, I wrote this book for the thousands of couples who have not yet conceived, and possibly may never have children biologically. My hope is that our story might encourage and persuade them to consider adoption as a possible option in their desire to parent. Angie and I are now strong advocates for adoption. It is a glorious and wonderful event. It's also an all-consuming and unpredictable emotional journey.

Fourth, I wrote this book to throw a beam of light on a masculine awakening, one that moved me into a profoundly different view of marriage and family life and, eventually, a career! Without any loss of my sports passion and competitive nature, I have become more sensitive, open, and vulnerable. I am glad that I spent the decade-long experience described in this book, though I would not want to repeat it! I'm a different—a more complete —husband, father, friend, and pastor.

To my beloved wife, Angie, who put her heart on the line for our two sons and then her life on the line for our two daughters; and who daily gives them and me all that she has in order to live out our dream of a complete family, I say thank you and I love you forever.

To our birthparents, Matt and Milli, who placed the precious gifts of their children into our hearts and our hands: You will always be a part of our family, and we will eagerly honor our commitment of an open relationship and will raise Eliah and Jacob with the love and sacrifice that matches what you did for us.

Finally, sincere thanks to all who stood by us during this journey—to all the friends we love and who know that we love them. And in particular, to Peggy Masching, Kay Currie, Lea Anderson, Phyllis Blizzard, and to our three immediate and extended families, the Elgin Evangelical Free Church; Calvary Baptist Church and Judson College.

Elliott J. Anderson

I. THE PROBLEM AND THE PRAYER

METRA TRAIN IN ELGIN

CHAPTER 1

Metra Messenger

It was a ripped and dirty seat in the last car of the ice-cold Metra commuter train, but it was the only one that was without another passenger in it, so I sat down and shivered. I quickly placed my backpack and my bag next to me to discourage any other last-minute riders from joining me. I held on to my shiny new plaque that announced my induction into my high school athletic hall-of-fame, and as the train pulled and jerked into motion, spontaneous tears began to slide down my cheeks.

They weren't tears of pride or happiness. Instead they were another uncontrollable and sudden release of my soul's sadness and emptiness due to the inability of my wife and me to conceive children for almost a decade. I leaned my head back on the uncomfortable metal bar that doubled as a headrest and dozed in and out of prayer and self-pity.

I don't know how long I was in that state, but I do know what woke me up. WHACK! Out of nowhere, I was hit in the back of the head with something that felt like a blunt weapon. Before I could stumble to consciousness it happened again, WHACK! I lurched forward and shot a quick glance over my shoulder as I raised my arms over my head in fear and confusion, sure that I was being mugged by some street hoodlums or gang bangers.

To my utter astonishment, the hostile attacker was a toothless, gum-smiling, middle-aged bag woman with about six sweaters on. A tattered old ball cap rested loosely on tangled and unwashed wavy, brown hair. Her right hand held a tightly rolled-up *Chicago Sun-Times*. She saw my look of horror and amazement and happily countered with, "How ya doing, honey?" Before I responded, I looked around to gain some context and composure and noticed that several other passengers were looking on with shock and amusement. "How ya doing, honey?" she repeated again, as if her head-smacking greeting was a normal form of introduction.

"Fine, until you hit me on the head twice," I offered nervously. "Why did you do that?" I asked.

"I just wanted to see how you were doing," she replied, sitting down in the seat behind me where I assume she'd been for the duration of the trip from Chicago's Union Station.

I sat back down in my seat, but this time faced her direction, still a bit unsure of my surroundings and her motives. "I'm OK, I guess," I stammered, hoping this would end the conversation and I could go back to sulking. No such luck.

"What do you have there?" she asked, looking at my Hall-of Fame plaque.

"An award from high school." I retorted a bit coldly, trying to communicate my displeasure at her intrusion.

She went on unabated. "Where are you going?"

"I'm going back home," I said, purposely void of city or destination.

"Where's home?" she responded, completely unphased by my verbal and non-verbal attempts to control the conversation.

I sighed and gave in, letting my guard down against my better judgment. "I live in Elgin," I told her. "I was at my parents' home in Cincinnati, Ohio, and I'm going back to Elgin where I live."

"I used to live in Elgin," she replied, and I couldn't help but wonder if she had spent significant time in the well-known Elgin Mental Health Center that was only a short distance from my current residence.

"Where do you live now?" I asked her, returning the intrusive manner of our dialogue. I thought I could at least turn the interrogation her way to avoid further disclosure—a standard counselor's trick for clients without boundaries.

"I live at the zoo," she said seriously.

"You do?" I said in amusement, and I couldn't stop a reactive smile.

"Yes, honey. I used to work in the circus and now I live at the zoo because I am comfortable with animals and can speak to them and play with them and they protect me," she declared with confidence.

By this point, a majority of the other passengers were leaning toward us in vicarious anticipation of the remainder of this comedic interaction.

I continued, now almost enjoying the attention and harmless banter. "What is your name?" I asked playfully.

"Mary," she happily volunteered.

"What's yours?" she countered fairly.

"Elliott."

The conversation went on for about fifteen more minutes, and we covered topics such as our family histories, our careers, and our distaste for the blustery winter wind that is so common in Chicago and its suburbs. Our voices had lowered and my defensive posture had relaxed, and to the disappointment of most of the other passengers, there was no further display of violence. Then just when I thought I had her in a comfortable realm, she surprised me again.

"Do you believe in God?" she asked softly.

"I sure do," I said proudly, and in one of those moments you pray for, I began to share the Gospel with her in a simple and direct manner. Pleased with my effort, I waited for her overwhelming conversion experience.

"I already believe all of that stuff, honey," she grinned with a twinkle in her eye. "But thanks for sharing. I have to get off at the next stop. Do you have $20?" she probed without hesitation.

Now it made sense. This was her routine. She had worked me all along waiting for the moment I let her in so she could then ask for money with a much higher probability of success. Whether an act or not, I don't know, but it was successful. I reached into my backpack, found my wallet, and looked in the billfold. Sure enough, all I had was a $20 bill. I pulled it out and handed it to her with an affectionate "God bless you" along with it. She beamed with contentment and then caught me off guard yet again.

"Can I pray for you?" she asked sincerely.

"S-s-s-s-ure," I stammered, now embarrassed by the once-again public nature of this conversation and the intimate gesture on her part. Before I could even bow my head or shut my eyes, she grabbed my hand, covered it with her own, and launched into one of the most holy and beautiful prayers I have ever heard in my life. After getting over my natural reaction to rip my hand out of her grasp and back away to a more appropriate distance, I shut my eyes, bowed my head, allowed the moment to be what it was, and relaxed into a spirit of prayer.

The content of the prayer included issues and insights from my life that no stranger, and certainly no bag lady, should have known or been able to discern in a 20-minute conversation. I don't recall all of the specifics of the prayer or where we were exactly on the route to Elgin when this incident happened, but

I'll always remember Mary, and I'll never forget the last line of her charismatic, flavored prayer on my behalf.

"And Lord, bless Elliott, bless his wife, and may all of his dreams come true. Amen." She gripped my hand tighter and looked me dead in the eyes, penetrating my soul; and held that stare of love and compassion until I looked away for fear of an emotional reaction. Then, as quickly as the whole ordeal began, it was over. She let go of my hand, slid into the aisle, seemed to float to the back of the train and disappeared into the night without so much as a wave or a good-bye glance.

I sat dumbfounded the rest of the trip. Was Mary an angel sent by God to give me hope? A hallucination? A vision? I decided I better ask one of the other passengers whether or not he had seen her. To my relief he had. I couldn't help but feel uplifted.

In fact, I had difficulty thinking about anything else that night, even though I had to coach my college basketball team against our arch rivals just an hour after I arrived home. Later, I had an even harder time sleeping as I replayed the Mary Mystery for my wife and then over and over again in my head.

Do you believe that God still speaks through dreams? Do you believe that God uses angels to deliver words of encouragement or hope? I do believe that Mary was an angel and I do believe that the Lord sent her to assure me of His plan for my future family.

10TH WEDDING ANNIVERSARY

Chapter 2

Dream Denied

My wife and I were married in the summer of 1989. I had just graduated from Judson College in Elgin, Illinois, and my wife, Angie, was teaching first grade in nearby Carpentersville. The unspoken, yet pre-determined plan for the next five years was for me to take two years to get an MA in counseling psychology, and then find a job counseling families with wild boys. After that, we would settle in and begin looking for a house. Finally, Angie would stop working so she could get pregnant, and we would start a family.

Does this sound familiar? Yes. It's a normal variation of the American dream. Get married, find jobs, buy a house, and start a family. It's as easy as one, two, three.

But then rarely does anyone anticipate fertility problems. At least nobody does out loud. Even if there is a family history of difficulty with conception or pregnancies, infertility is rarely a topic of conversation, even among close friends. It's just never discussed prior to it being an issue, partly for fear that by speaking of it, it might actually come to pass.

We never talked about it. Ironically, when we did decide to try and get pregnant, I made the poor choice of announcing it in our family Christmas letter of 1992. That anticipated Christmas blessing ended up on back order for the rest of the decade!

I grew up in a strong Christian family. It was a very stable, loving, social, and extremely active, even boisterous, environment. With a professor father and librarian mother, few topics were off-limits; but I can't remember ever hearing about a couple who had problems having children.

This is despite the fact that my neighborhood best friend and his sister were both adopted, yet I still don't remember ever discussing it with him, his family, or my family even once in our entire childhood relationship. It wasn't a scary issue or a forbidden topic. It was deeper than that. It was as if the adoption didn't exist at all. It was a closed adoption all the way around.

This was in the early 1970's and nearly all adoptions were still closed at that time. A closed adoption means that an adoptive couple is not permitted to know the identity of the biological parents. At that time in the process, adoption agencies were not allowed to legally release confidential files, and adopted children and the adoptive parents had no access to this information.

In my opinion, more often than not, this practice of closed adoption wreaked havoc in many homes. I saw this first hand when another friend, during her late teens, wrestled with her identity and adoptive child status. I remember the agony her mom went through as her daughter desired to locate her birthmother, or, in her words, her real mom.

I don't blame anyone for the impression all of this had on me; I just know that it was mostly negative. The result was that I viewed adoption as a secretive, risky, and difficult endeavor that would likely bring pain and confusion to the whole family. I think most of the kids I grew up with felt the same way—even the ones who had been adopted!

As a result of this perception, I used to tease my sister that she, too, was adopted. Looking back, I realize my intent was to project onto her exactly what I assumed adoptive kids always felt. I wanted her to feel fear about her place in the family and about her heritage and genetic link to the Anderson name. I hoped she'd feel insecure and uncertain regarding our family system. How cruel!

It's interesting that even as a young boy I was aware of the stigma associated with adoption and was trying to use it to my advantage. My sister and I laugh about it now, but how many other siblings in America have done something similar? I don't think my family's perception of adoption was much different from that of most people.

Well, the American dream for my wife and me was not completely missed, because I did get my master's degree in the regular two-year period, and shortly later began my first job as a crisis family therapist at Wheaton Youth Outreach in Wheaton, Illinois, primarily counseling wild boys.

One of my responsibilities as a crisis intervention therapist was to advocate for troubled teens. I worked with a program called the Minors Requiring Authoritative Intervention program of Illinois (MRAI). A disproportionate number of these families, at least on my case load, happened to be adoptive families. This simply confirmed my notion of the risks and turmoil associated with adoption.

A decade later, and thanks to some perception-shattering experiences, I believe adoption is one of the most wonderful and God-honoring processes a couple could ever experience. How did I change my opinion so drastically?

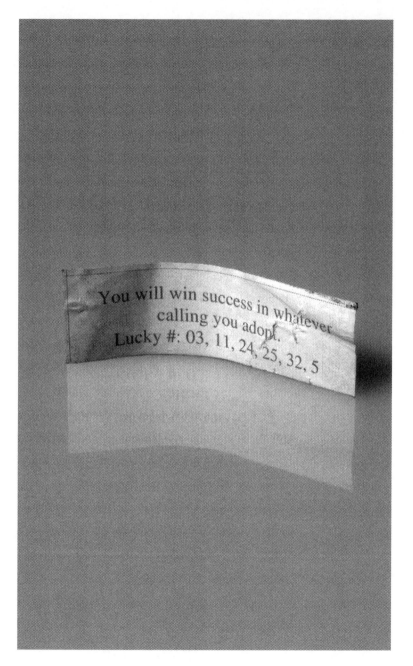

You will win success in whatever
calling you adopt.
Lucky #: 03, 11, 24, 25, 32, 5

FORTUNE FOR THE FUTURE

CHAPTER 3

Fortune Cookie

Sometime around 1997, after five years of unsuccessful conception efforts, we accepted the obvious, and began a quest for children through infertility treatments. Along the way we had tears of pain, sadness, relief, and joy, but no pregnancy. Three different gynecologists told Angie that she was one of the healthiest women they had ever examined. I don't know if that made us more frustrated with, or more reliant upon, God's will. Probably both.

We took the basic tests and followed all the procedures and never felt totally hopeless or defeated, partly because the doctors kept telling us we were fine, but there were sure seasons of high frustration! For a while we used Chlomed, one of the drugs known for stimulating egg production. We de-stressed our lives. I started wearing boxer shorts more regularly, and we improved our eating and exercise regime. In addition, my sperm count was tested twice. Both times it was fine.

The first time I had a sample tested was a rare humorous

moment in this ordeal. On the way to the hospital lab, I made a quick turn at an intersection, and the jar and the bag that was holding it rolled off the passenger seat and onto the floor. All of the contents spilled inside the brown bag. For some reason, when I arrived at the hospital, the lab worker didn't want to handle the bag, so he had ME walk it back to the lab! I could tell by their smiles and stifled laughter that I had just provided them a great "what happened at the office today" story.

The process of infertility testing itself, however, is anything but funny. After seeing and feeling the repeated blank stares from doctors, I couldn't decide who was more bothered by our failure to conceive—them or us. Though doctors desire to help, their focus on the end result can lead to aggressive and insensitive interactions. On top of all the other disappointments, we felt that we had disappointed our doctors, too. And that energy didn't help. It's a very emotional process for all parties involved. We're talking about creating life!

We did, of course, try all the suggested positions, timings, temperatures, and magical sexual conception strategies. This makes the entire sexual arena take on an intense level of importance. Spontaneity and passion are often lost since the desire for a child can outweigh the physical desire for your spouse. An attempt at conception becomes an event on the calendar, and sexual intimacy, as a result, often suffers.

I think we did fairly well in this battle, however, mainly

because our commitment to the marriage was already established, and it held a higher priority than our determination to become parents. This took a lot of self-examination and willingness to be vulnerable with one another, and that was beneficial to our relationship; but we certainly would have traded that growth opportunity for an easy conception.

By the spring of 1998, I was beginning to get very restless. I was tired of losing a game we knew we didn't hold the power to win through our own efforts. I wanted to parent, even if it meant raising exotic gerbils or hairless hamsters. Angie didn't feel the same urgency, which really surprised me because she was entering her mid-thirties. This is normally a difficult age for barren women as they realize they might never bear children biologically. More than once from 1997–1999, this difference in perspective led us to some late night (or all night) heated discussions, and one of the reoccurring issues that left us in turmoil was the question of adoption.

Within a period of about six months, I had dramatically changed my thoughts on adoption. And to be honest, initially, it probably had more to do with trying to fill the void than it did with actually choosing a path. Regardless of the motivation, by the time I had done some research and talked with a few adoptive parents, I was sold. So despite my irritation with her hesitancy, I didn't blame Angie for being cautious or apprehensive.

Our marriage survived and grew stronger because of this crisis.

However, I can see why infertility is one of the leading causes of divorce. The tension and pain are excruciating and the need to place blame can be deadly. I'm not sure if it was an act of strength or surrender, but after many difficult nights, we quit focusing on pregnancy all together. We focused our energy into other directions. If it happened, it happened; if it didn't, it didn't!

In the summer of 1998, we ended our six-year stint in a male dormitory as resident directors at Judson College. About the same time we purchased a big 19th-century Victorian home about two miles from the campus. The majestic old home needed some work, and we immediately turned our attention to its restoration and repair.

Home improvement projects proved a great infertility distraction. As we plunged into refurbishing our symbolic nest, we felt something close to the essence of our marital dream—which was for us, to have a family.

I can't tell you how many times I worked outside and thought a lot about children, or the lack thereof, while doing the tasks at hand. That vigorous physical activity was both productive escape and emotional therapy.

"Let's see now, first I'll clean out this old shed. By now, I should have a five-year-old son helping me clean out this shed. I'll have to mow that big back yard soon. It would be perfect for a playground or a neighborhood soccer game. Angie's making homemade pizza and chocolate chip cookies. Angie ought to have a six-year-old daughter helping her make those cookies. That old barn will need a new door pretty soon. Maybe I'll put up a basketball hoop up over the door."

Finally, in the middle of July, 1999, shortly after returning from our 10th wedding anniversary cruise, I'd had enough of the passive mindset and behavior. It is not our normal style of thinking or doing, and I couldn't take it any longer. I issued a decree in the land of family Anderson and told Angie that we were going to pursue adoption! This was not, and is not, the normal decision-making process in our union. Our marriage has been from the beginning a definite team approach.

We have what Yale professor and author Robert J. Sternberg describes as a "garden marriage." We are most comfortable when tackling goals and projects, but because we both like to lead, conflict and tension often emerge. Interestingly, we feed off this energy. My former boss once said, "You guys make a great business team, but the marriage must be difficult." He meant that as a compliment, and we took it as such. His analysis was right on.

Angie is excellent with finances and serves as the CFO of our household. She manages to get about two-thirds of our entire household needs (groceries, toiletries, cleaning supplies) for free. Her coupon and rebate organizational structure is more elaborate and complex than my budget spread sheets were at the college. Her nickname is "Bulldog," and her strong presence in the classroom when she taught was often "off the leash" at home as well.

We are both highly opinionated, so sometimes even minor household decisions play out like a courtroom drama.

We actually like to argue. I'm all passion, charm, and soft manipulation, while she's a tough and logical litigator who attacks my emotional presentation with calculated precision. Though we actually enjoy the more-than-occasional sparring, during our season of infertility, we avoided serious fights because there was way too much buried sadness and anger. So my decision to move forward on adoption without her full blessing was unusual.

Since the beginning of our marriage, Angie and I had considered lots of "family" options. My work in crisis therapy led us to talk seriously about opening our home to some type of nontraditional parenting. We had discussed foster parenting, group home supervision, and a variety of other community service possibilities. Then we began to try to get pregnant, moved into the dorm at Judson, and became very confused about the future of our family.

It's ironic how the reality of a situation changes your perception of what is acceptable, what is alternative, and what is a concession. Most people don't like to concede. We like to choose. To make matters more intense, Angie and I are both very competitive. In the early stages of exploring adoption, our drive and perfectionism caused us to see adoption as "second best." Up until the time I made the decision to schedule our orientation meeting, adoption had run the gamut for us—scary, undesirable, alternative, last resort, and then . . . a concession. Now, I wanted it to be a choice. And the right choice!

After much prayer and many long conversations with God, I began to feel a strong sense of His direction. I asked one of my student workers at the college to get on the Internet and find a group of adoption agencies to consider. I did all this without Angie's knowledge, and I didn't have the slightest idea when or how I would break the news to her.

Angie has a way of letting everyone know when things don't go the way she thinks they should, and I wasn't sure I wanted to push this issue more than I already had. The more I read about adoption, though, the more excited I became, and the more peace I felt about the decision. I was moving forward and knew she would eventually join me, but I wanted it all to happen with her blessing, not her reluctant acceptance.

In order to break the news in a safe way and to stay within the soft manipulations of my personality, I took Angie out to her favorite Chinese restaurant. I brought her brother, Brock, along as reinforcement and a buffer. He was a student at Judson at the time, and often hung out at our house, so it was comfortable and normal to have him join us for a meal. I had shared with him my intention so that he wouldn't be shocked at the announcement.

As gently as possible, I slipped the "big" news into our general conversation while Angie leisurely enjoyed her egg drop soup.

"Angie, I've been looking into adoption agencies, and I want to move forward on this process."

Brock and I locked eyes for a brief second and held our breath in suspense. She actually took it much better than we had anticipated. I think the public disclosure was a wise approach—this time.

She didn't say anything at first, but began to cry softly. Finally, she responded in typical Angie style with a list of highly detailed questions about the agency, the timing, and the cost of the process. Being a big-picture thinker, and knowing that my wife approaches life in specific and orderly details, I had studied the materials thoroughly so I could present a reasonable number of facts and assure her of my confidence in this move.

Her ability to analyze a lot of information "on the fly" astounds me, and, as usual, she absorbed the material quickly. Her demeanor and spirit let me know that I finally had her nervous blessing. I was glad I had taken the time to do my homework and thankful God had softened her heart prior to the decision.

The sense of relief was enormous! Finally, the walls of defense around the entire adoption process were tumbling down. What at once felt like "second best" we now believed to be a possible blessing and reasonable "choice." When we ended our meal, the waitress brought us our fortune cookies, and in a typical moment of spontaneous silliness for me, I declared that my fortune would be extremely important to our marriage.

I opened the cookie, read the fortune out loud, and our laughter stopped abruptly. It read, "**You will win success in whatever calling you ADOPT.**" Chills went over my whole body. Brock's jaw dropped. Angie stared in disbelief. Can you believe that fortune?!? First, Mary on the Metra, now the fortune in the cookie; were these coincidences or was God at work in our future?

We sat in silence for a moment before opening the other two cookies. We read the fortune again and again, feeling the excitement and energy of a special family memory with a touch of the Holy Spirit at the same time. We went home with full stomachs from the buffet and a new sense of hope in our hearts.

The next step in the adoption process for us was to inform our parents. Both our mothers had also dealt with long seasons of infertility, so they truly empathized in our plight. Besides tearful reminiscing of their own barren years, they felt the insecurities all mothers feel when their children's deep desires are unfulfilled. They celebrated with us when we told them the great news. Finally, we felt as if we had some control in the ordeal! We could put some of the longing and yearning into action.

II. EXPLORING ADOPTION

WHEATON YOUTH OUTREACH, WHEATON, ILLINOIS

CHAPTER 4

Confirmations

When we began our adoption process, I prayed specifically that the Lord would reveal that this was the right thing to do at the right time in our marriage. The following moments of confirmation may seem minor and trivial, but almost all adoptive families can relate to the need to feel direction and peace about the overwhelming experience. These kinds of confirmations are regular occurrences in the adoption market. In fact, I think they are in all areas of life, but the raw vulnerability of the adoption process makes you more in-tune and in-touch with these providential "coincidences."

As our peace in the decision grew, we sensed that God was in this journey, that He had always been with us, and that we were walking in His will. We were obedient, not because adoption on its own is an automatically holy event, but because our lives were faithful to His Word and our choices were guided by His principles. Sometimes God's will is no more complicated than that, even when the result of obedience is not necessarily automatic happiness or fulfillment of dreams.

The adoption agency I had chosen was Sunny Ridge Family Center in Wheaton, Illinois. The first meeting happened to be devoted to international adoptions. It was an interesting night, but there was no excitement in the car as we drove the forty minutes back to Elgin.

The decision to adopt had been daunting enough on its own. The thought of now needing to choose a specific country was too much for us. Therefore, we ruled out an international adoption for the first go around. So, a week later we attended the domestic adoptions meeting. It was exactly what we had hoped it would be, and this time there was an intense feeling of anticipation between us on the return route. When we were home, we skimmed over the materials and began to lay plans for our approaching family. This time, unlike previous late-night heart and soul sessions, the plans seemed tangible and realistic.

Early the next evening I dove into the entirety of the Sunny Ridge domestic adoption packet. The official application form was two sheets of paper, four sides, and it asked for a staggering variety of comprehensive and very specific details, the "we are naked and not ashamed" kind of self-disclosure. As I worked through the questions I realized that we could not possibly move forward without revealing our souls and I wondered how Angie, a natural introvert, would handle this semi-public vulnerability.

We had to provide all the traditional personal information (name, address, phone number, age, national heritage, occupation, and such), of course. Then income level, infertility status, plans for child care after placement, and any medical or psychological problems either of us might have had and how we solved them. I didn't really know how to communicate that God had intervened in my life and now used all of my chaotic personality issues for His glory! It was not easy stuff, regardless, even for a counselor who is a natural self-discloser.

The application continued with questions on smoking, drinking, and overall mental health. Next, was a request for an account of our religious affiliation, membership, practices, and plans for the child's religious instruction. Finally, there was a probe into our feelings about a completely open association with the birthparents. This was our first face-to-face confrontation with open adoption, and it was intimidating to read these questions and answer with such little understanding or context. Here is an example of some of the questions and our immediate answers.

1. Would we be willing to meet with the biological parents? (Yes.)

2. Would we accept gifts and letters from them? (Yes.)

3. Would we share pictures with them and send letters to them after placement? (Yes.)

4. Would we accept a child of a different race from ours? (Yes, but with discussion.)

5. Would we accept a child born to a mother who had no prenatal care? (Maybe.)

6. Would we consider a baby born to a mother who had used drugs and alcohol? (Not likely.)

This is just a sample of the questions, and clearly they are thorough and carefully designed to help determine important mental perceptions and intentions. It wasn't evident then, but now I can understand why these questions are so challenging so early in the process. You must handle the intense interrogation at the beginning, so that you will be able to sustain during the pressure of the actual placement.

The application form explained that even after placement, responsibility for the baby would move from the birthparents, to the court system, and then finally to the adoptive parents. We hadn't realized that it would take several months before everything was legally secure. This was also unsettling. Images of CNN and well-known "Whose baby is it?" dramas flashed through our minds.

Then around page four, they hit you with the financial details —another harsh reality. It started with a non-refundable application fee of $200. If accepted, the total cost of adopting a child was

$15,500. This included the medical costs for a normal delivery for the birthmother and the baby. In comparison to the cost of a biological delivery, this is not really expensive, but insurance handles 80 – 90% of that bill for most couples. With adoption, it is cash in hand, and these figures are already seven years old!

The last statement of the application form stripped us of whatever minuscule amount of control and power we had left in the entire arrangement. It stated, "If you have the combined characteristics that our birthmothers most often request, we will contact you to begin the formal home study."

What do they mean, "**IF** we have the combined characteristics . . ."? Wasn't all of the information I'd just provided enough? Don't tell me that even after I'd exposed our inner selves they still might decide that we are "unfit" or "inadequate"! It seemed so unfair! Who questions the unwed nineteen year old about her plans for the future, her financial status, and her readiness for parenthood? And it is not just teenagers sowing their wild oats that have surprise conceptions; some say up to fifty percent of pregnancies within marriages are still unplanned. Where is the agency requiring all expectant parents to go under scrutiny and investigation like this?

And then, if they deemed us "worthy," how much more invasive could the formal home study possibly be? I was already telling the agency everything they needed to know to make a reasonable judgment about our character, lifestyle, and parental worth.

Really, what else was there to know that couldn't be gleaned from the initial application?

Our caseworker, Becky McDougal, fielded my frustrations and defended the rationale for the interrogation. Sunny Ridge is very selective in whom they accept as adoptive parents. They have no more than thirty clients on profile, and they strive to keep a balance between religion, race, age, socioeconomic status, and other demographic factors that reflect the general population of their birthmother clients. This is fairly standard practice at evangelical agencies. We had been told very early in the process that we were good candidates. We were relatively young; we were financially stable; we were educators; we were Christians; and most importantly, we were willing to consider an "open adoption."

This gave us an expectation that our application would be accepted promptly and settled my defensive posture. After waiting two agonizing weeks to hear anything further, we braced ourselves for another round of grieving, and my anger boiled once again! After three weeks without an answer to our application, we assumed the worst; we'd been rejected by yet another parental judgment! Was something seriously wrong with us as individuals, as a couple? Maybe we weren't supposed to be adoptive parents either?

This dashed hope took us to the brink of permanent retreat! Was God shutting the door to parenthood once and for all? What could have been so wrong with the application? Did I come on too strong about our personalities and our commitment to the Christian faith? I was tired of wondering and second guessing. We were both seriously wounded enough. Neither of us wanted to say it out loud, but accepting a childless existence was close to the surface. To attempt to take our minds off of the pain, Angie and I escaped to a Friday night dinner and movie.

It didn't work! Releasing your mind from deep pain is nearly impossible. Sometimes, something seemingly minor or insignificant will trigger an emotional response that leaves you defeated or exhausted for days. Other times, the trigger is more obvious, like the recognition of moms on Mother's Day. Those kinds of tears are nearly automatic. Then, an off-hand comment from a colleague at work devastates you for a week!

Neither Angie nor I remember what movie we saw that night. On the way back home we lamented the rejected application in a manner which nearly all infertile couples know too well—we attacked each other! We were venting at the whole world and indirectly at God. I wasn't soft in my manipulations that night and Angie wasn't reserved in her retorts. It was exhausting and emotionally draining. Normally after one of these altercations, we would just go our own way for a while once home. This time we didn't get the chance to sulk!

In typical fashion for us, as soon as we got home, I went to get something to eat, regardless of when I had eaten last, and Angie went to the bathroom regardless of when she had gone last! I put the keys on the island and started to fix myself a bowl of cereal. On her way to the bathroom, Angie hit the message button on the answering machine to see who had called. We both paused to listen. After several familiar voices, we heard someone we didn't recognize—a message that would change our lives forever.

The voice was Arlene Betts, the director of adoption services at Sunny Ridge. She had been in Ireland for two weeks and had just returned. Apologizing profusely, she explained that Sunny Ridge had accepted us into the adoptive parents program, but in her absence had failed to let us know!

I put down my spoon in disbelief; there was complete silence in the house. I ran to see how Angie had reacted. She was still seated and still stunned! On top of that joyous news, Arlene wanted to know if we could start the adoptive parenting training sessions the next Monday night! This was almost two months ahead of the normal time schedule. From rejection to advanced placement in two minutes! I called her back immediately, though it was almost 10:00 PM and asked her to give us one day for prayer as a matter of spiritual formality, but I knew our answer was already guaranteed. "YES!" "YES!"

The next morning I rushed to the phone, ignoring my own self-imposed 24-hour waiting period. Joyfully I accepted Arlene's invitation. If they would have allowed us to, I would have camped out on Sunny Ridge's front lawn for the rest of the weekend! Only an act of God would have kept me from that meeting Monday night!

There are more fascinating and amazing confirmations ahead in this story, but none of them was as important as this one. Arlene's message had both crucial timing and a significant impact. We were just about to give up the dream when God called to remind us who was running the show.

The second confirmation took place that Monday night at the first group meeting. We arrived ten minutes early and took two seats near the front. The chairs were arranged in two rows, classroom style, all facing the front of the room where a podium was standing. The room was abuzz with anticipatory tension that was neither happy nor sad.

Arlene Betts, our new best friend, was in charge, and she was very warm and gregarious. She did a great job welcoming the couples, most of whom, like us, were in a slight state of shock. We all huddled close to our spouses and responded courteously and appropriately, but without depth or emotion.

It was kind of like visiting an AA meeting (something I did for an addiction counseling class in grad school). You don't look around too much. You don't stare at anybody, and you generally keep to yourself. Your shared pain and experience gives the group an automatic bond that doesn't call for icebreakers or facilitation. Once the meeting starts and all the people are seated, there is an instant, but silent camaraderie felt by all.

It's probably the same at every veterans get together across the country. No matter where you were stationed, how you got there, or how you made it home, you were all in a war. The fertility legionnaires are no different. The veterans in our group sat taller and straighter in their chairs, clearly signifying their status as the experienced ones, and then willingly and proudly told their stories for us boot campers who had just joined the ranks.

At the first break, I heard a familiar voice behind me. I turned around and saw my friend, Scott, a guy I played pick-up basketball with at Judson. "What are you doing here?" I asked, realizing instantly it was a dumb question.

He laughed and told me that he and his wife had adopted all three of their children from Sunny Ridge, and that they were considering, once again, adding to their family. From general sideline conversation in the gym, I knew he had several kids. It occurred to me that nobody had ever asked, and he had never mentioned, that his children were adopted. It gave the whole adoption concept more normalcy for me.

We talked at length after the meeting and agreed to car pool to the next few sessions. Scott and his wife then also gladly offered themselves as mentors. We loved hearing their story and listening to their positive experiences about Sunny Ridge and their adoptions—and in particular, about the "open" aspect of their relationship with their birthmothers. This led to the foreshadowing of a third confirmation, because the first kids they adopted from Sunny Ridge about eight years prior ... were twins!

OUR VICTORIAN HOUSE IN ELGIN

Chapter 5

"Open" Education

Angie and I are genuinely "open" people; we have visitors and friends in our home almost daily. When resident directors at the men's dorm we lived by an "open door" philosophy. In addition, we've had thirteen different people live with us for varying lengths of time. I imagine we will relate in this spirit of "openness" for as long we live.

"Open" adoption, however, was a brand new concept. Even after we had researched it, we were still somewhat naive as to how the arrangement would actually take place. We had a hunch that it was a good thing for both couples, and, more importantly, we were pretty sure of the emotional and psychological benefits to the children. But, we still had much to learn.

Sunny Ridge requires all adoptive couples to read *Dear Birthmother*, by Kathleen Silber and Phylis Speedlin. This collection of letters from adoptive parents to birthparents, and vice versa, is an important educational lesson and a very moving emotional experience. Any couple considering adoption and especially "open" adoption should read this book. You will almost assuredly identify with at least one or two of the letters, if not many. We quickly passed the book among our family and friends, and bought a few additional ones about open adoption for further study.

As beneficial as the reading and research was, nothing sold us more on the open process than hearing from some actual birthmothers in person.

During the last of the group meetings at Sunny Ridge, we heard from a panel of birthmothers. We were excited about this opportunity to learn from actual birthmothers, but we were also apprehensive, knowing that their stories would soon be our reality and their pain would now be quite relevant and soon absorbed into our future. On the panel were several recent birthmothers who shared with us both the joy and loss of placing their children for adoption. Overall they were at peace with their decision, and the process, and comfortable with the families who had received their babies. This "live" affirmation of the positive nature of open adoption was most reassuring, and it gave us a tangible point of reference for what we were about to experience.

The birthmom who was the most influential, however, was a middle-aged mother who twenty years ago had not been involved in an open adoption. The difference in her story compared to the stories of the other birthmothers was dramatic, as she told of the years of agony she went through knowing absolutely nothing about her daughter. She said it was as if her daughter had died. The lack of any information made closure and growth almost impossible.

Now, after twenty years of silence, she had located her daughter, and they had met recently for the first time. The reunion was a healing occasion for both, and an opportunity to start a brand new, yet difficult, relationship was about to be explored. The look of relief and release was clearly visible in all her non-verbal communication.

This particular meeting was a pivotal moment in my trust of open adoption. With two degrees in psychology, and being an avid reader of psychological material, I felt I now had a grasp of the benefits of openness for both family systems. After her talk, however, I began to consciously "own" openness. I was no longer the counselor learning another therapeutic technique; I was now the hopeful father understanding the benefits of an open system. Now, both Angie and I could become strong advocates of open adoption, explaining the concept to others with boldness and confidence. We moved through our fear and embraced openness as our own.

After riding the pendulum swing both ways, I'll summarize the reservations couples experience when considering adoption, and in particular, open adoption. Really, it comes down to one word—fear. Fear of the vulnerability. Fear of not being able to truly love "someone else's" child. Fear of the child's dual identification. Fear that our parents might not want to be grandparents to "someone else's" child. Fear that the biological parents might become too possessive as time goes on. Fear that the biological grandparents will intrude. Fear of our own inadequacies as caregivers. Fear that the child might grow to adulthood and then reject us. Fear of fear itself.

Most of the couples who have gone through infertility procedures know first hand how gripping and paralyzing fear can be. Most of us can look back, years after a successful adoption or a biological birth has taken place, and wonder why we didn't pursue alternative options sooner.

Embracing open adoption involves wrestling with an immediate contradiction. It means sharing intimate experiences with the very people who decided that they couldn't or shouldn't be responsible for those exact same experiences. To the new and nervous adoptive parents, this often feels like a concession of control and security. How can we allow the birthparents to continue to see their biological child and still develop a safe and protective environment? For mothers, I think, this fear is even more territorial. She might think, "Wait a minute. This woman placed her baby with us, and now my maternal instincts are telling me to prevent anyone else from bonding with my child."

As a father, I had my concerns as well. For example, how could my children have another father they might identify with and probably look like, yet spend their whole life completely free from his influence and guidance? Would my future daughter run into the arms of her birthfather with the same speed and energy as she did mine? Would my future son want to "hang out" with his birthfather more than with me?

What if the birthmother changes her mind or disagrees with our parenting style, and takes us to court with charges of neglect, abuse, or endangerment? How would I respond in twenty years if my son told me that he wished he had been raised by his birthfather instead of me? Would my heart ever heal from that kind of blow? These questions, and many more, are understandable and reasonable, and they definitely need to be processed verbally and cognitively with your spouse, your caseworker, and your family for two very important reasons.

First, we must understand that the most critical aspect of open adoption is, indeed, the word *open*. And the key player in this openness is not the birthparent or the adoptive parent, it is the child. Of course, when proper communication and structure exist in an open adoption relationship, there is no doubt that both parental units are greatly positively affected. This does not come close, however, to the need for the child to feel a strong sense of belonging, identity, and heredity. And the child can only get that complete picture and gain that security and stability if the entire process is in the open. How open and what that openness means to each family can certainly vary, but the opportunity for an adopted child to know his/her history is as important as it is for any one else.

Openness removes the stigma and the fantasy element for an adopted child who knows his own background, his placement circumstances, and his complete historical being. When open adoption is explained as a natural occurrence, it is neither frightening nor bizarre in nature. Children of an open system are able to discuss the relationships that have determined and will continue to determine their lives, with all the parents in their family system being fair topics of conversation.

The children do not get to choose who their birthparents or their adoptive parents are, but now, with an open adoption, they can choose to explore for themselves how to process the nuances and individuality of their particular situation. It allows them to be more than just adopted kids. They are special, chosen children who use adoption vernacular such as *birthmother* in a way that gives their lives credence and their story validity. Telling their adoption story then becomes familiar and comfortable. It is simply the uniqueness of their own family.

Second, we must understand that a majority of our fears are self-protective and reactionary. We are concerned with how we will feel and how we will handle possible rejection. We are afraid that the birthmother will not like us, while she is most likely worried that we will not like her. It is human nature to become self-absorbed and self-conscious under pressure and stress. This is taken to an even higher level when we are talking about exchanging the parental rights of a vulnerable, defenseless, and helpless little baby.

The birthparents are usually already feeling a certain level of shame and guilt for their decision to place the baby for adoption. And they wonder if the adoptive parents will sense how guilty they feel and judge them for it. Meanwhile, the adoptive parents often believe that the birthparents will not like them, and will decide to keep the baby or will give it to another couple once they see how pathetically vulnerable and powerless the adoptive parents really are.

It is a vicious cycle of self-doubt and insecurity, which leaves the precious gift waiting tenderly in the balance. But the cycle serves as an important part in the child's future, and I believe children have the right to learn about their parents' feelings and fears.

This is why for decades society chose to avoid this contradiction altogether, as if the woman who gave the gift of her child was not worthy of a return gift of openness and inclusion. How can we justify such selfishness in the wake of her undeniable unselfishness?

There is no doubt in my mind that open adoption is, in a majority of non-crisis adoption placements, the healthier and wiser choice. I pray that you would be open to open adoption!

NEW YEARS EVE, 1999, IN CINCINNATI, OHIO

CHAPTER 6

Disclosure Profile

Another area of fear for adoptive parents is the home visit. The investigative nature of this process is unnerving and uncomfortable. As a former crisis therapist, I too had visited families in their homes in the midst of pain, conflict, and fatigue. It felt almost like my former clients had gained a vicarious retribution since I was now the one being examined. I could understand some of their defensiveness more clearly than I had before.

Instead of feeling defensive, however, I felt burdened and put upon that Angie and I had already spent more than 150 hours on this project, and yet here we were again answering another round of questions and filling out more forms.

Why does a couple dying to have a child have to prove first to the agency, then to the state, and finally to the birthparents that they would be worthy parents? Meanwhile, a couple who really doesn't want a child can bring one into the world without so much as a raised eyebrow from their neighbors, much less the county, state, and federal government. It certainly is a strange contradiction to internalize and really feels unfair.

There are two main components to the home study. The first involves a visit by the social worker where you must provide the following information:

1. Copy of our marriage license.

2. Copy of divorce decree (if applicable).

3. Copy of pet inoculation certificate.

4. Copy of well water inspection (if applicable).

5. Copy of wage stub or income tax return.

6. Copy of birth certificates.

7. Fire evacuation plan and smoke detectors.

8. Proof that all dangerous weapons, tools, drugs, and household supplies should be out of reach of children.

9. Measurement of the child's room.

10. Health insurance benefit book, for reference.

The second part is the creation of the couple profile and the "dear birthparents" letter. The profile and letter are comprehensive written documents that will be shared with prospective birthparents. I liken this experience to giving your personal testimony when you join a church. You want to be sincere and forthcoming, while putting your best foot forward. And you certainly don't want your "weaker moments" to be what everybody remembers on the way home from the service and discusses at the next church picnic.

I was even more apprehensive about the profile after our caseworker told us how birthmothers sometimes select adoptive parents based on random details. For example, one birthmother chose her prospective couple when she learned that both couples had spaghetti dinners every Friday night. Another one selected her adoptive parents because they enjoyed chasing ambulances and fire trucks, just like she did! Therefore, disclosing some microscopic part of your personality or character, or even a tiny bizarre habit, could be the single factor that determines the birth-mother's choice.

Realizing this strange fact was both liberating and paralyzing. Which tidbit should I add to our profile? Should I admit that since childhood I have been obsessed with the Cincinnati Reds and my mood is often affected by the outcome of even a regular season game? Should I confess that back in high school I once had a warrant for my arrest when I accidentally skipped a court case involving a reckless driving and drag racing charge? Or, should I disclose on the positive side and brag about the time and service we give our friends and family?

After much prayer, I chose a direct approach for our profile, very up front about what we are like as a couple, and how we planned to parent their child, and sprinkled with less dramatic disclosures. And since Angie and I wanted to have a relationship with the birthfather, as well as the birthmother, I addressed our profile to both.

Here is the letter.

Dear Birthparents,

The gift of life is the greatest gift that God bestows on humans, and you are about to share that gift with others who have, for whatever reason, been unable to receive the gift biologically. This choice you will soon make will alter our lives (yours and ours) dramatically, and at the same time connect us forever. Thank you for your willingness to look outside yourself and consciously choose a selfless path for your child. We on the receiving end of the gift are indebted to you for your sacrifice.

Angie and I are in our early thirties and have been married for ten years. We've been trying to have children for seven years and have recently felt inclined to consider adoption. When we made the commitment to pursue this route, I took Angie to a Chinese restaurant (her favorite), and told her that I had called Sunny Ridge and scheduled our first orientation meetings.

I then told her that the fortune in my fortune cookie would be important to this endeavor (I often say things like this to keep conversations interesting or playful). After I read the fortune out loud, we were both silent for a moment. It read, you will win in life in whatever calling you adopt.

I include this story in our profile to give you a glimpse into our marriage and personalities. We are devoted Christians who trust God with all our heart, soul, strength, and mind. We also love our neighbors as ourselves. These are the two greatest commandments according to the Bible, and we base our lives on these principles.

I had been praying for many months about the adoption issue, and asked for some kind of sign that it was the right decision for our marriage. Who knows? Maybe the fortune cookie was confirmation that we were walking down the right road. Regardless, I believe that it is God's will for us to adopt a child from Sunny Ridge, and I feel that the birthparents who choose us will experience peace knowing that we are the right couple to parent their child.

I am Vice President for Student Development at Judson College, a Christian liberal arts school in Elgin, Illinois. Angie is a first grade teacher, who has been working part-time because we spent six years as resident directors in a male dormitory on campus. Interfacing with the college students until 2 AM, and then teaching first graders all day, was an impossible task. So we reduced Angie's teaching load so she could be a part of both worlds.

My job entails supervision and control of all student activities of the college. We have just over 800 traditional students, and I am their advocate in the college administration. I have a master's of psychology degree in counseling, and I worked as a family crisis therapist before I started full time in an educational setting.

I enjoy counseling, but working with college students is more holistic, as I can become involved in their lives beyond a fifty-minute session in an office. I am also responsible for all the student discipline in the school. Because of my own tendency to test the limits and boundaries of policies and procedures, I am familiar with the attitudes and behavior that come my way. I enjoy the opportunity to help mold the lives of students.

Angie and I were both surprise children to our parents. Angie's mother was sixteen when she was born, and her mom faced many of the same challenges and societal pressures that some of you may be facing now. The difference is that thirty-five years ago the entire process was purposefully kept quiet and isolated. As it happened, later, it took Angie's mom fifteen years before she got pregnant a second time.

In my mom's case, she stopped menstruating three years after my brother was born. She went to her doctor to find out why, and after the examination, the doctor informed her that there was nothing to do—because she was pregnant (with me) at that very moment. Infertility is not a foreign issue in our family system.

Angie and I are active and driven people. One of our displays of cooperation is working. We both love to accomplish projects like yard work and home improvement tasks. Angie is skilled in traditional household matters like cooking, sewing, crafts, laundry, and baking. She credits this foundation to her grandparents, who helped raise her while her parents finished school. Angie and I read a lot—Angie on health issues and on home finances, and I on psychology, leadership, and spiritual formation. I also enjoy playing the drums and participating in competitive sports. I have coached college baseball and basketball over the past several years.

Neither of us enjoys idle time, but we look forward to settling down with the addition of a baby in the house.

Our siblings live in the Fox River Valley also, and they are very involved in our lives. My younger sister, Karin, is in her second year of doctoral studies at Northern Illinois University in the field of developmental psychology. She comes from DeKalb to Elgin at least once a week to visit us.

Angie's younger brother, Brock, is a freshman at Judson College. He has stayed with us in the summer during the last seven years. He lives in the dorms now and will not be living with us this coming summer, but visits our home often.

My older brother, Warren, teaches English at Judson College, and lives adjacent to the campus. We have a lot of interchange with his family—wife, Lea, and children, Amie, age 6, and Austin, age 5. For a while, Warren and Lea were resident directors in one of the girls' dorms, so we spent hundreds of hours bonding with Lea, Austin, and Amie.

My parents live in Cincinnati. My father is a college music professor and my mother is a state clerk and librarian. She taught high school until my older brother was born and then did not go back to the classroom until my baby sister was six years old. They come to Elgin two or three times a year, and we visit them in Cincinnati on holidays.

Angie's parents live in southeast Iowa, a little closer to Illinois, so we exchange visits more frequently with them. Angie's dad owns his own contracting firm, and her mom helps out with the family business, works part time in an optometry shop, and is an occasional beautician on the side. Both sets of parents are still together. My parents just celebrated their 41st anniversary and Angie's parents recently celebrated their 34th. Divorce is not a pattern anywhere in either side of our family.

There has been a previous positive adoption experience in our genealogy. Angie's biological grandfather, on her dad's side, left his young wife and two small boys, ages 1 and 2. Angie's grandmother remarried, and her husband, Miles, adopted the boys and raised them. Miles was not only a great father to the boys, but also was and continues to be an excellent grandfather to Angie, Brock, and now to me.

It is wonderful to witness and experience, first hand, the purity and completeness of his love for our family, and to know that we will model that in our generation. We plan to use Miles as the middle name for our first boy, and the fact that our first son will be adopted is a beautiful and appropriate circumstance that honors Miles.

Friends are very important part of our lifestyle, as well. Since we've lived close to the school and been involved with Judson College for fourteen years, we have many former students who live in the area. Our church has about thirty alumni in the congregation, and we meet every other month with a group of our former resident assistants.

I am still close to three of my high school friends, and I'm in constant contact with three of my college roommates. Angie's best friend from Iowa lived with her in Elgin before we were married. Tragically, however, Angie's friend passed away three years ago from brain cancer. Angie relates very well with males, so she joins me in the mentoring and counseling of the college boys.

Adoption is not a second-tier decision for us. It is part of the plan for our lives and our future. We have no reservations about this process. I could not be any more excited if Angie were pregnant herself; the only difference is the lack of a normal nine-month timeframe to our waiting. We know that we will be good parents, but we're realistic about the world and the nature of children. There will be mistakes, bruises, tears, and accidents, but we will give the rest of our lives to care for all the people the Lord has allowed us to love—our children, our wonderful family, and our friends.

May God be with you in your selection process.

Elliott and Angie Anderson

There it is. This is who you are, what you are about, and what you hope to be. The birthparents out there who might consider you, however, are still a mystery. And they hold your hopes and dreams in their hands.

Another challenging consideration is to pre-select which possible difficulties or handicaps you are willing to accept in an adoptive child. Suppose the baby, to everyone's shock, is of a different race, or is born addicted to crack cocaine, or suffered permanent brain damage during a troublesome delivery, or is born deaf or blind. Will you, the adoptive couple, follow through on your agreement?

The need to make such decisions is obvious, but Angie and I wondered if we declined an imperfect baby, would we miss an opportunity or blessing God intended for us? We selfishly hoped we wouldn't have to face one of those kinds of decisions!

In hindsight, after going through the difficult year of disclosure, analysis, and probing, I believe it would be beneficial for all would-be parents to prepare in this way. In fact, I currently use many of the questions and worksheets of the home study in my pre-marital instruction. The home study process did what it was supposed to, and we are better parents because of it.

III. THE ADOPTION ANSWER

INITIATING THE OFFENSE, JUDSON COLLEGE POINT GUARD, 1988

CHAPTER 7

Selection Monday

In December of 1999, we received our official Foster Care License from the State of Illinois Department of Children and Family Services. The excitement was building. Now, all we had to do was wait.

Wait. Yes, just wait. Waiting is different for adoptive parents-to-be than for biological parents-to-be. There is no absolute nine-month timeframe for us. We'd heard stories about young birthmothers who changed their mind and refused to part with their child. We'd heard stories of couples who waited two or three years to get a baby. We'd heard all kinds of heart-breaking stories that had occurred in situations like ours. Angie and I had no idea what might be in store for us.

The waiting, at least initially, was tough, but certainly buffered because we were too busy to dwell on it. I was still coaching two varsity college teams, basketball and baseball, and serving as

Vice President for Student Development at the college, in charge of eleven different areas of student services.

As it happened, when school started back in September, I entered my basketball team in a Christmas tournament in Cancun, Mexico. The *Tourneo de Basquetbol* turned out to be an ideal diversion for taking our minds off the waiting game.

Angie was still teaching part-time, but did hundreds of things for us as a couple and for my teams, booking and arranging this basketball trip, for example—air line tickets, hotel accommodations, financial arrangements for meals, time schedules, bus travel to and from the hotel to the sports event, free time for sight-seeing and shopping, and such.

Then, of course, at every step along the way something went wrong. Airplanes were late or overbooked, hotel rooms were incorrectly assigned, the entire group was split in two different hotels, local bus schedules were unreliable, conference rooms for my pre-game team meetings were not available at the right times, the sports arena was six miles away from our living quarters, and on, and on, and on.

As a player and a coach, I'd been on many such sports trips before. But this one felt different. I felt as if my parenting career had already begun. It was merely a waiting game now.

And, incidentally, it was a huge crowd to take care of; around sixty people went with us! We had invited a lot of friends and relatives—my parents, my sister, Angie's brother, my old college roommate, several sets of parents of the basketball players, and my assistant coach and his wife. In addition, the women's team and their extended families also made the trip. It was a big occasion, more like a Judson College community outing than a sports event.

During this whole time in Cancun, Mexico, Angie and I did not have time to think very much about the adoption proceedings back home. During the trip, however, we were living proof that a great way to deal with the anxiety in a childless marriage is to give to others. This giving, and in particular, this giving to high-energy college kids, filled the void in our lives and gave us a chance to influence and shape young adults who were under our care. And part of this shaping was being real with the students about what we were going through. They were part of our rooting section and had seen my emotions about the process first hand.

I'd learned about grief in my academic studies when I was training to be a psychologist and counselor, and now I was learning about it internally, first hand; and proactive grieving is almost always more healthy than reactive solitude, as long as the grievers are dealing with their own emotions and not simply burying them in exchange for serving others.

Four months after the Cancun basketball trip, on a snowy and cold night in April, the waiting and the grieving were both still there. This particular night I was watching Michigan State and Florida battle for the NCAA basketball championship. I was in my usual sports-watching position on the love seat, with a Gatorade (I too needed to replenish electrolytes during the contest) and a variety of quasi-healthy snacks. Angie was sewing in the living room, mending her brother's boxer shorts, and feigning occasional interest in the score or my theatrics.

It was halftime when the phone rang. It was a fast-paced game and I was, of course, in a hyped-up mood. I'm a passionate sports fan, so my friends know not to call during big games, especially end-of-the-season games like University of Cincinnati basketball, Cincinnati Reds baseball, Ohio State football, and Chicago Bulls basketball. So I had a hunch the call was from a stranger or from one of the other coach's wives or NCAA tournament widows!

Because I was so focused on the game, I didn't recognize the voice or even acknowledge our case worker's, Becky McDougal's greeting. She carried on in communication anyway! After then exchanging some brief pleasantries, Becky asked me how I felt about parenting twins! She went on to tell me some more details about the birthparent's situation, timing, and the preparation needed for placement, but all I could think was, "We have been selected and the babies were twins!"

As Becky continued with her general instructions, I looked into the living room and noticed that Angie had stopped sewing and had her head in her hands. She had overheard my near-yelling-level conversation and had always wanted twins. It was too good to be true!

Becky concluded her joyful information and then asked if I had any questions. I said no, but asked if she would repeat every single piece of this news all over again to Angie. She gladly agreed and Angie went to the kitchen phone for the best phone call of her life! I stumbled back toward the love seat, but stayed on the cordless phone to hear Angie's reaction to the news.

Once again, the timing involved was fast and furious. We were not only selected, we were scheduled to meet the birthparents the following Monday, April 10th! Becky answered a few more of our excited and fairly impulsive questions, and after a few more minutes we hung up the phone. Angie stayed in the kitchen and then immediately called our family and closest friends while I returned my attention to the championship game.

Contrary to my normal viewing habits, though, now I sat for the entire second half and barely moved a muscle, my manic energy repressed and contained. But it wasn't focused concentration on a well-played game. Uncharacteristically, I can't even recall any of the statistics or the final score. I just stared at the TV, smiling, with tears rolling down my cheeks, knowing I was finally going to be a dad.

SUNNY RIDGE FAMILY CENTER, WHEATON, ILLINOIS

CHAPTER 8

Meet the Birthparents!

My siblings and I have been performing in public since we were little kids. All of us are very comfortable speaking, teaching, singing, or acting in front of large groups of people. As a drummer, I've performed in front of hundreds of people hundreds of times. As a coach and athlete, I have played in front of capacity crowds under huge demands from screaming fans. I have a lot of nervous energy before public events, but I'm not fearful or timid. I enjoy the spotlight. It energizes me.

Socially, I'm at ease with all varieties of people—rich or poor, strong or weak, male or female, black or white, outgoing or timid, loud or quiet. I'm telling all this to deepen the significance of my next sentence: I was scared out of my mind to meet the birthparents. I had enormous cognitive, emotional, physical, and psychological fear of that first meeting.

The weather approved of our special night. It was a cool, crisp, but sunny evening as we drove the 25 miles to Sunny Ridge to meet the birthparents who had selected us. We talked about the bizarre nature of the evening. We were going to meet two young people who were young enough to be our children—and they were going to decide in a two-hour forced social gathering whether they wanted to give us their children! This is the kind of adoption thought paradoxes that can drive you crazy if you let them. In hindsight, it would have been better if I would have shut down my analytical brain for the day.

On the more fun side during the ride, we struggled to decide what our ideal combination of twins might be. Would we do a better job with two girls, or two boys, or a boy and a girl? If two boys or two girls, did we want identical or fraternal twins? The speculation was exciting because we had no idea what sex the babies were.

We also struggled because we noticed that our normal personality dynamics were completely reversed. I dreaded the meeting convinced, that I would come on too strong or too hyper and would overwhelm the couple with my "presence." Angie was as calm as could be and was glowing with positive energy and peace. She felt that this was our special couple, and she was brimming with optimism. Her confidence made me all the more nervous as I imagined her heart being broken when the birthparents decided to select another couple with a more "normal" husband and future father.

Then I carried the runaway fatalism even further by projecting that when these birthparents did indeed reject us, Angie would be angry that I ruined the interview and would take our names off the profile list. Worse yet, we would stay married, but Angie would shut me out of her life. She would hold me responsible for the botched meeting, and she would turn into a nagging and bitter spouse for the remainder of our lives on earth. You see what I mean about needing to turn that side of my brain off for the day?

As we parked the car and meandered toward the front door, I had a very strong impulse to run into the woods, or pretend to be hallucinating, so Angie would decide she was better off meeting the birthparents by herself.

This was often the mental state I was in just before the start of a big game, as I considered all of the ways I could blow it for our team. When the game started, though, I shift into a different person. I block all of that negative random energy out and lock into a sustained focus on defeating the competition. Then, because I had already imagined the worse, I am at a positive peace level and can play without fear of the result. There was no such game that night, however, and I prayed earnestly for a supernatural calmness to come upon me.

When we were inside the facility, I blurted something out to Angie and escaped to the men's room to try to gain some composure. I splashed cold water on my face, did some deep breathing, checked my breath and the fly of my trousers, and stepped out into the hallway. Angie was losing patience with me, but still had some sympathy in her eyes as we grabbed hands and headed up the stairs. I was about to meet the two young people I needed more than I had needed anyone since I committed my life to Angie in marriage eleven years before. I am still amazed that she followed through with that event, so there was hope for this occasion as well.

We reached the upper floor landing and the building was eerily quiet and dark. The meeting room was at the end of the hall. The corridor was almost pitch black and absolutely silent. Were they just sitting in the room listening to our approach? Would we walk into the wrong room and meet the wrong couple? What if we liked the wrong couple more than the couple we were supposed to meet? In a moment of humorous self-deprecating relief, I said out loud to myself, "Dead man walking"—a quote from the movie of the same name. After a biting glare from Angie, I passively followed her into the room where we would meet our long-awaited future.

Most of us, in moments of real honesty, admit that physical attractiveness is important to us at some level. Even if we recognize our own imperfections and have come to accept them, we reprocess our own adolescent identity when we envision our future children. All this speculation is, of course, a complete waste of time, since genetics determines a large percentage of the outcome.

If you are an adoptive parent, it is even more pointless to worry about the "looks" of your children because it is completely out of your control. Still, Angie and I were both hoping for an attractive couple—and the moment we saw them we were relieved, and then more than relieved, we were impressed.

The birthmother, Milli, was fairly tall, had strawberry blond hair, Scandinavian features, green eyes, and a warm smile. She was obviously nervous, but seemed to be genuinely excited to meet us. She actually reminded me a great deal of my sister, Karin, a very attractive Nordic beauty in her own right.

The birthfather, Matt, was about the same height, but had dark hair, dark eyes, and handsome Italian features and coloring. I told myself I wouldn't do it, but I imagined the combined characteristics of the birthparents, and instantly concluded that their twins, our twins, would be good looking.

Becky, our caseworker, opened the official conversation, then quickly dismissed herself after the communication began to flow smoothly. I took that as a sign that she was confident that things would go well. It wasn't quite a miracle, but I did manage to be on my best behavior, avoiding the tendency I have when nervous to overly use humor or self-disclosure. I also made sure that Angie had many opportunities to reveal who she was and how she would mother the babies. After all, Matt and I were secondary, at least in initial reads, in this equation. This was a woman-to-woman and future-mother-to-future-mother evaluation, despite their difference in age of almost twenty years.

Sometimes in marriage you experience moments where you are so proud of your spouse that you fall in love all over again. This meeting was certainly one of those moments for me. Angie was incredible that night. She was respectful and appreciative of the birthparents and their decision, but was not the least bit condescending or patronizing. She was composed and confident. They seemed to be as impressed as I was. There was a lot of small talk mixed in with the more serious questions, and after a half-hour or so, I was convinced that this was a match made in heaven.

About fifteen minutes later, Angie asked Milli if she knew the sex of the twins. Milli had actually just found out herself and was proud to tell us that they were boys. We couldn't contain our smiles and outward expression of joy and admitted to them that two boys was by far our first choice for the gender of their children. (As if we would have walked out of the room or told them that if she would have said two girls!) I am sure we would have been just as happy no matter what combination she would have revealed, but it did make it more spontaneous and genuine that two boys was indeed our preference.

Then Milli really surprised us and took out a long list of questions that she, or they both, had prepared for us. This was a great sign for me because it showed that she had prepared for the meeting. She did not appear to be making an impulsive or random choice. We hoped that bode well for the future.

Her questions ranged from the simple and silly, "What are

your favorite pizza toppings?" to the serious, "What does your faith look like and how will it affect the boys' upbringing?" She raised other relevant questions, as well, like "How are you preparing to parent twins?" "Will Angie stay at home with the boys?" "Will Elliott push them into sports and music?"

When we had satisfactorily answered all of the questions on her list, I copied the mood, and asked in return, "How do you perceive the future relationship of all four families—mine, Angie's, Matt's, and yours?" They discussed their desire for openness, but also expressed some reservation about the extent of that relationship. Once again, this was nearly identical to the way that we felt, so this helped us establish another bond in this precarious dance. This part of the conversation went on for another forty-five minutes or so, at which time Becky reappeared and suggested that I close the meeting with a prayer.

As we were walking out of the room, Milli requested an additional meeting quickly so we could meet her mother. Talk about your blessing on departure. We gladly accepted this affirmation and the return trip to Sunny Ridge was scheduled just two days later. No waiting this time! We knew we had passed round one!

The corridor and stairwell were somehow much brighter and even festive on our way down to the lobby. Finally, on the way home, I could release my manic energy. I am sure I drove her crazy the next three hours talking non-stop! If I remember correctly, Angie was pretty talkative that night, as well!

ANGIE AND SUSIE ON OUR WEDDING DAY

CHAPTER 9

Another Mother-in-Law?

The relationship with a mother-in-law is one of the most complex relationships in a family system. It is also a frequent topic for stand-up comedians, which usually means there is plenty of truth and pain in the relationship. My relationship with Angie's mother is very good now, but it was not an easy transition. In the eighteen years of this process, I've learned a few things about that relationship and am much wiser because of it.

First, a good mother commits twenty years or so of her life to her children's immediate needs, mostly at the expense of her own needs, and the remaining years of her life she wonders how well she did that task. Therefore, she has a substantial and lifelong investment of time, money, and emotion in the human being she helped shape. Suddenly, twenty or so years into that process, a different human being, an outsider, and often a complete stranger swoops in for the wedding and enjoys the future from all that hard work the mother put into the task.

Second, a good mother tries to avoid this, but she often has a few of her own personal unfulfilled goals wrapped into her adult child. A marriage brings a young spouse on the scene that may or may not care about those unfulfilled goals of the mother. And the mother knows that this new spouse will soon have far greater influence on her child's life than she (the mother) ever will again.

Third, a good mother is fiercely protective, and would willingly lay down her life for her offspring. Will her child's spouse do the same? Most young couples, partly because of age and immaturity, and partly because they don't know any better, enter a marriage with their primary concerns being selfish only. It usually takes a minor crisis or two to test the newlyweds to determine what kind of relationship they really have and whether or not it is worth the unconditional acceptance of the elder in-laws.

In addition, she must now call this intruder "son" or "daughter," even though she has had no opportunity to shape this person's life. Now she is forced to blindly trust that somehow this new couple will reflect enough of her own personality and family traditions so the last twenty years won't be lost in the formation of a new family unit. That's a lot of baggage to sort through, and it is totally unavoidable. In fact, the stronger the family, often the harder that separation is.

Thanks to my years of experience in this realm, I was more confident about meeting Caroline, our new mother-in-law, and suffered no similar psychological or mental meltdown. Angie and

I were both excited by the chance to get to know her. Our eagerness was heightened by the fact that we had been told that she had been the one who had steered Matt and Milli towards our profile in the first place!

It was obvious, therefore, that Caroline had some significant power in the family system, so I was intrigued by the chance to witness that influence. The meeting reminded me of my old crisis intervention sessions where the family power structure will be revealed one way or another. My job then as counselor was to make a quick analysis of the power grid and to propose some alternatives to the maladaptive behavior. I was geared up for therapist observations, and my senses were ready for action.

We met in a different room this time. The mood was much lighter. Milli welcomed us like an old friend, and I could tell she was anxious to show us off to her mother. The format for the meeting was almost identical to the first. There was small talk and informalities, and then there were more intense questions with more weight behind them. I could tell that Caroline was impressed with Angie's package of traditional skills.

Then, just when I felt we had passed round two with flying colors, Caroline pulled out her own detailed list of questions. I was disappointed in myself that I had not been ready for this maneuver, as she probably helped her daughter prepare the previous list for the initial meeting.

As she reached into her purse to retrieve her list of questions, the silence signaled the magnitude of our approaching responses. Angie and I glanced at each other quickly and inquisitively. I figured I'd take the same path as I had in the first meeting and make sure that Angie took the lead on most of the responses. I assumed that this woman needed to test my woman to make it to round three.

The first question, however, was directed at me. She asked, "What will you say to Jesus when you get to the gates of heaven that will make Him say, 'Welcome my good and faithful servant'?" Now, for most committed Christians, this is not a difficult question, especially if it is just in casual conversation. But, in this case, the question shocked us, and for a moment, I froze!

There was a long and dreadful period of complete stillness. Caroline gazed at me intently. I finally gave Angie an "I'm going to nail this one" look, offered a silent prayer for guidance and wisdom, and then spoke with confidence. I told her that there was nothing I could say to Jesus to make him say anything because my salvation is all because of His grace, and I would acknowledge His sovereignty, His authority, and His glory.

Caroline did not hide her pleasure with this answer, and the whole room let out a collective sigh of relief. I think I dropped about three pounds sweating in the one-minute experience and Milli gave me a non-verbal "high-five" with her eyes!

There were many more interesting questions, like "Angie, what is your favorite flower?" Angie responded with a lilac, because it reminded her of her paternal grandmother's house. Then she added peonies, because they reminded her of her maternal grand-mother's home where she used to pick big bouquets and place them in centerpieces.

Who was making the sales pitch, now? Angie was brilliant. Her answers paid respect to both of her family lineages, and at the same time symbolically welcomed Caroline into our future. I asked Angie about her responses later, and she said all the deeper meanings and messages were providential. She had just answered with some justification.

More questions followed. "How are your eating habits? How would they change with children? How will you institute good eating habits with them?" We responded that we were healthy eaters and not prone to diets or fads, and that we believed in exercise and nutritional supplements. We also projected no big change in our food patterns when the children were at home because we were not a fast-food, carry-out, or eat-on-the-run couple. It was soon evident that Caroline, an orderly, list-making grandmother, was greatly pleased to learn about Angie's logical and systematic approach to homemaking.

Financial matters came next. Caroline asked specifically, "How much debt do you have? Do you have a good savings plan, in particular, one that would provide a college education for the twin boys?" It was an important question for sure.

First Angie described our household budget, laying out the organization, structure, and benefits of the system as if she were giving a seminar (which she has). Milli and her mom were both impressed. Then I explained that as a college administrator all our children will be eligible for free college tuition within the Council of Christian Colleges and Universities (CCCU), an organization that includes around one hundred schools in America. There were many more questions and responses, but these three areas are sufficient to provide an idea of the thoroughness and extensiveness of the meeting/interview.

As she had at the initial meeting, Becky came in after about an hour and asked me to close in prayer. Just like on Monday, Milli asked us on our way out the door if we wanted to join her and Matt at a local restaurant that coming Sunday night. We had passed round two!

The foundation of the relationship was being poured. It was really a period of infatuation, bringing back memories of second and third dates in high school when the romance builds at a surreal pace. Of course, we quickly agreed despite plans that would have to be changed.

We agreed on a time and place and then departed to our cars. On the way home, Angie and I had a feeling that God's will was unfolding before our eyes and it was almost too much emotion to process so quickly. After all of those years, the pace of the movement now was like a *Star Trek* movie—warp speed!

The dinner on Sunday went very well. We discussed the names of the boys (they had chosen Nicholas and Alexander, and we had chosen Eliah and Jacob). All four choices were historical and imperial, which I thought was profound. We talked about the relationships of the extended families and the future of both birthparents after placement. Matt was much more relaxed in this atmosphere, and we began to get to know him also.

The meal was excellent and the conversation was comfortable. We really enjoyed each others' company. It was by far the most unorthodox double date either couple had ever experienced. On the way home, the fatigue of the week hit us, and by the time we pulled in the driveway we were ready for a good night's rest and really didn't discuss the week any further. We were confident that we had passed round three!

Round four turned out to be another meal. This was my kind of family! Milli had requested the meal so that we could meet one of her sisters, Meredith, so we asked if we could bring my sister, Karin. The roots were spreading and the extended family was being ushered into the open adoption family system.

We sat family to family—Angie, Karin, and I on one side and Milli, Caroline, and Meredith on the other. Matt was not able, not invited, or chose not to attend. This informal and neutral atmosphere helped both parties be at home. We felt accepted and confident enough to really be ourselves, and it seemed that they felt the same way.

For the first time, I began to show a little of the quirks to my sense of humor by repeatedly razzing Caroline when she accidentally drank from my water glass. There we were, two families sharing food, laughter, and fellowship. Two families bound together forever by this beautiful but strange circumstance. Two precious baby boys would be born in two months, and these three women were going to give those boys and all of the rights, duties, and privileges that pertain to that covenant to us. Astonishing! Amazing! Several times during the meal, I would spontaneously choke up with emotion, and I tried to hide the tears that welled up in my eyes.

Several other attempts to meet with Milli and Matt fell through for a variety of reasons. One time, Milli had the flu. Another time, I had a last-minute need to attend to at Judson. And so, after four quick and spontaneous meetings in a two-week period in April of 2000, we did not see Milli, Matt, or the rest of their family during the remaining two months of the pregnancy. It was unfortunate, but understandable, so we didn't give it much thought. Later, we wished we had forced the issue.

THE BOYS' ROOM

CHAPTER 10

The Waiting Game

Milli's due date was in late June. My most demanding responsibilities at the college came to an end around Mother's Day. Summer was busy for us, but a much more relaxed state. Now that our parent timetable had an end date, we figured we had better start preparing for its arrival.

We had never taken the step to decorate a baby room before. Many infertile couples do and I can understand the excitement and the positive anticipation, but we had also heard the other side of that move—that the room becomes a painful reminder. Now, with just about a month left to wait, we felt it was safe to create one.

Angie and Brock came up with the nighttime theme of a moon and stars. The colors were a couple of different shades of blue, with yellow accents. Brock sketched out sixty-three different sizes of stars all over the walls and ceiling, and then added a large smiling moon on the ceiling. For the walls, we chose a soft, off-white blue, for the ceiling a traditional white, with stars of either navy or Carolina blue. The moon, of course, was yellow, and with the help of Pottery Barn and Target, the bumper pads, coat rack, and rugs followed suit.

Another part of the traditional waiting game is baby showers. My college and Angie's grade school held showers for us before the placement and adoption were final. This is a little premature and risky, but we did it to be sure of good attendance before summer vacation scattered everyone. We'd both been employed at our schools for a decade, so there were many close friends who wanted to share our joy of finally becoming parents. They had been such huge supportive influences during the journey; we figured the risk was worth the appreciation and connection.

Both schools flooded us with gifts and love. I remember looking at all the baby toys, some of which I had no idea how to put together, and thinking to myself that even two boys couldn't possibly make use of all this stuff. We had our mini-van packed to the limit on both evenings, and began the never-ending battle of how to appropriately organize the storage of all those children's things.

Despite the celebrative moods, however, there are still some difficult emotions for an adoptive parent during a baby shower, especially if it is before the actual placement. It is a challenging mix of joy and fear tangled with a disturbing guilt that comes to the forefront more often than you would like. The guilt is twofold and I think intensifies based on the number of barren years a couple has experienced.

First, there is the internal guilt you still wrestle with for not being able to begin your parenting life the "normal way." Because most adoptions in America take place as a result of infertility, this is a natural association. And no matter how hard you try to dismiss this guilt, you still can't avoid the feeling in the back of your mind that you had to "purchase" your child, and all your friends didn't. This is not the kind of guilt that makes you angry or leaves you feeling dirty. It is the kind of guilt that is more closely linked to sadness and disappointment.

Second is the sense of pity you detect from others. There is a fine line between empathy and pity, and adoptive couples are very sensitive to that boundary. It's wonderful to be loved, cared for, prayed for, and to experience the comfort of your community. It is another thing to suspect that the group feels sorry for you. When you sense that you are a "charity couple," and that people feel sorry for you, the gifts and the hugs take on new meaning, and you may find yourself questioning the sincerity of the delivery.

Most of these thoughts and mind games are unfounded, but they are still there and will often gnaw at you. Thankfully, neither of our school relationships cast that shadow on us, and any feelings we had in that direction were limited.

The more awkward moments in the wait communication period usually come from those who know you well enough to be included, but don't know you well enough to know some of the inner thoughts. For example, many people are caught off guard by the intensity and complexity of adoption, and speak out carelessly as they attempt to grasp the full ramifications for an adoptive couple. You hear questions like, "I'm so happy for you and Angie. Do you think it'll be hard to raise somebody else's kids?" or unsolicited and untrue warnings such as, "Make sure you don't have an open adoption because most birthparents end up taking the children back."

Another common example is the questions about appearance. "What if the boys don't look anything like you?" This is an understandable question when contemplating the complexity of adoption, but is really silly in nature. "Well," I would sometimes answer, "we will probably have them undergo plastic surgery until they do resemble me." Now, of course we wouldn't do that, but it was fun to see their surprised reaction! What do they do if one of their biological children doesn't look like either one of them? They love that child with all their heart and praise that special little one for being unique.

I could never anticipate what I might say when these questions came up in an otherwise congenial conversation. I always felt uncomfortable with the innuendo suggesting that I might be sorry, someday, trying to rear a non-biological child. As I look back now, I realized I developed various defense responses to reframe the language of the question, to deny the point outright with a return question, or to simply change the topic. No matter how, when, where, and why you adopt, adoptive parents must prepare for and learn to handle these kinds of questions and comments. It is part of the process.

By the time June rolled around, the excitement and anticipation was reaching a crescendo. We had worked through the details of the birth with Milli several weeks earlier, so we were not in a constant state of ready departure or anxiety on that particular matter. She desired a private time of closure with her family after the birth, and the least we could do was respect and support that decision, which we did. The placement was to take place at Sunny Ridge a couple of days after the boys were born.

Around my birthday, June 3rd, Milli called and told us that she was starting to dilate. We promptly called all our immediate family and then waited anxiously by the phone. Unfortunately for us, and more so for Milli, she continued in that partially dilated state and went back and forth to the hospital for almost two weeks.

Then, a decade of infertility for Angie and me came to an end in another dramatic confirmation from God that He had planned for us to have a family this way all along. Nicholas and Alexander (Eliah and Jacob) were born on June 17, 2000, the exact date of our 11th wedding anniversary! Eliah weighed 5 pounds, 8 ounces, and was delivered at 7:58 PM. Jacob weighed 7 pounds, 4 ounces, and was born at 8:04 PM.

I've never felt such a strange and powerful feeling of vicarious happiness. I was joyful, but emotionally confused! I was ecstatic, but somehow couldn't really celebrate. My heart would not release all of the emotions until the boys were actually in my arms, in my house, bearing the Anderson name. Would it happen soon? I was caught off guard by my own reaction. Angie just cried a lot—mostly happy tears.

We knew we had to wait for that privilege of physical contact, however, and were content to call our families and tell them of the birth. Later that day, we got the call we were waiting for. Becky called from the hospital to inform us that the placement would take place either the next day, Sunday, June 18th, or Monday, the 19th—just a day or two left in the decade long journey!

The call, though, changed the waiting period for me. The deadline was here. The time to transition was now! It took everything in my power not to jump into the car and drive down to the hospital to catch a glimpse of our sons, even if I had to go incognito to do it. The remainder of the night we frantically roamed around the house with nothing substantial or important left to do.

Sleep was not easy for me that night. The feelings and thoughts were reminiscent of the night before our wedding. You know your life is about to dramatically change, but you really have no idea exactly how until you experience it. So, you just imagine it all and waver between exhilaration and nausea—and your heart beats so fast and hard it resonates through your whole body!

ANGIE AND GRANDPA MILES HENDERSON

MY PARENTS, NANCY AND SIMON AT JUDSON BASKETBALL GAME 1999

Chapter 11

Placement Day?

We didn't hear a thing from anybody that Sunday until almost 5:00 PM As you can imagine, that was like an eternity for us, and we were not happy with the delay. Throughout the many months of the entire adoption procedures, we had respected both the birthparents' need for privacy and the caseworkers' need for professionalism. Because my former crisis therapy clients were often disrespectful of client/therapist boundaries, I knew these frustrations from the perspective of the professional. Therefore, I had never pushed Becky about anything.

By noon on Sunday, however, Angie and I were so filled with fear that something had gone wrong that I broke my own principle and put in several calls to Becky's pager. None were answered! Finally, late in the afternoon she called to explain that she had been in downtown Chicago all day on another case. She said she would check in with Milli as soon as she got back to her home in

Wheaton. Her lack of information both bothered my conscience and my sense of professional etiquette.

This confirmed the very principle I had violated. I'm sure Becky did not want to see our phone number constantly flashing on her pager as she worked with another family in Chicago. I'd been there. It's distracting and interferes with your work. Nevertheless, just hearing Becky's voice calmed our hearts, and helped us through the rest of the day. I guess in that context, as my previous clients probably had felt, I was glad that I had called and figured it was her job to take care of me!

Milli and Angie had done the direct communicating during the past few months, so there seemed to be no need to alter that pattern now. We did, however, allow Becky to be the facilitator during this series of events, as Milli had been telling Becky all of her placement plans. We continued to stay back in the client role in what felt like an odd third-party scenario now that the boys had been born.

Each slowly passing hour was excruciating. When it felt like something must be wrong, Becky called Sunday evening to confirm our fears. She said that Milli and the babies were doing well, but Milli had not determined the exact day of placement, moving the date now to Tuesday or possibly even Wednesday. Milli was enjoying her brief time with the boys, and she wanted to soak up as much mothering as she could while they were still in her possession. We were really sad, but certainly understood; and how do you counter a mother's desire to love her boys a few more days before she gives them to you to raise forever?

Monday turned out to be a tough day from start to finish. Knowing the boys were entering their second full day of life out of the womb, and we had yet to see them, began to feel a little strange and inappropriate. Not being at the birth was one thing. Being held at bay while the birthparents bonded with the boys was another. It just didn't feel right based on all of the previous planning and discussions, but we were helpless and left to our own growing fears.

Part of the reason we wanted an open adoption was to be an intricate part of the whole birthing event (selection, birth, after-care, placement, birthdays, holidays, celebrations, and such). We knew it might be awkward at times, but we wanted to be included in everything from the very beginning. We had agreed to the privacy and closure at birth, but believed that the time for us to be involved was now! My anxiety level was off the charts and it kept climbing as the day went on.

Shortly before noon we received a call from Becky telling us she had further bad news. Bad news after a friend or colleague has been on a hospital visit is usually more than bad news. It is often fatal news. Angie answered the phone with a traditional greeting, and then remained silent for what seemed like an hour. I felt like I'd been run over by a bus when I heard her voice crack, saw the tears roll down her cheeks, and watched the color leave her face. I wanted to scream and knock something over, even though I didn't know exactly why yet. I just stood there frozen and in shock.

For reasons I'll never understand, I didn't pick up the other phone to listen, perhaps because I didn't want to hear what was being said. I think I was afraid of my own feelings. Then, as Angie hung up the phone and collapsed on the couch, I found myself instinctively switching modes from angry adoptive dad to crisis therapist. My professional training kicked in and I buried my fear and anger to get control of myself. If I wouldn't have, I am sure that long-healed violent tendencies would have surfaced, and our living room furniture would have been the victim of my explosion. My wife needed a strong and loving man, not a weak and impulsive one—so I buried my instinct and desires and sat on the couch and held her.

Between sobs and tissues, Angie explained that Milli and Matt had had a terrible fight the previous night at the hospital. She kicked him out of the room and was now in a state of huge emotional turmoil. She felt she could not lose Matt and the boys in the same day. She said she would call Becky tomorrow to decide about the future.

Decide on the future? I thought the future had been decided months before! The future was now! The future was right here! The future was supposed to be at our house in our arms! We had planned for this future for over ten years, and now, just because the birthparents had a lovers' quarrel, our future was once again somewhere else.

Though it was not a termination of the entire possibility, it sure felt that way. It was like learning your girlfriend had cheated on you, but wasn't really sure yet if she really wanted to break up! You have hope still because your love for her is still there, even though the initial pangs of betrayal have dropped you to your knees!

I had a knot in the pit of my stomach now that was squeezing the life out of me. I literally started to have trouble breathing. This couldn't be happening. I begged God to not allow this placement to fail. I was too angry to be heartbroken, yet too sad to remain passive. After giving Angie as much quiet couch time as I possibly could (probably twenty minutes though it felt like two hours) I got up and fretted and paced around the house like a madman. I was vacillating between hope and despair impulsively doing push-ups and sit-ups to try and alleviate the mounting kinetic energy that wanted a destructive release.

By the end of the day, all of Angie's optimism and confidence had vanished. She stayed on the couch off and on for about eight hours. She was fully grieving the loss that I wouldn't, or couldn't, acknowledge existed yet. Angie cried continuously, sometimes hard, sometimes soft, and sometimes in short burst as she mentally played out the agony of a dream suddenly taken away. I simply remained silent, and after a couple hours of frantic-hyper stalking about the house, I sat on the couch with Angie and didn't move for hours.

As is often the case in times of high stress or strain, spouses mentally balance each other's perspectives. Angie thought it was done—a failed placement. I could not allow myself to go there yet, if for no other reason than because she was already there. Even though we both knew the ratio of placements that fail after birth was very high (some say as high as 50%), I did not believe that this one was over yet. I held on to the dream, and silently remembered what I had observed about Milli's family.

Her mother, Caroline, had hand-picked us as the right adoptive couple, so certainly she would calm Milli down and talk her through this understandably enormously emotional, hormone-driven, impulsive decision. Matt would come to his senses, and apologize for whatever he needed to apologize for (what man hasn't been there before?), and we would work this all out in a day or two.

I called Becky myself later that night and rehashed the entire episode. We talked, professional counselor to professional counselor, about the prognosis. Becky didn't make any false promises or give any hopeful assurance, and she agreed with me that the final call was still in the balance. She told me she would continue to work with the family and would update us as soon as she detected any change in the situation. I was glad I had remained calm and appropriate, but what in the world were we supposed to do now?

Where do we go from here? We felt so alone. We didn't think we should tell too many people about the problem, but at the same time, friends and family were sure to start calling—and soon. We couldn't hide. We needed to release some kind of news to our loved ones.

We decided to call a few key people (our parents, our pastor, the president of the college) and explain the situation so they could pray for us and also so that they could give a statement to the communities that they led to request some privacy during this traumatic moment. I still believed we would get the boys somehow, but I had no idea whatsoever how it would come about and when it might happen. Angie was taking a darker path. She believed the adoption was over. We were a failed placement and would be another statistic for the records. How I hoped she was wrong! How I begged God to change Milli's mind!

JUDSON COLLEGE STUDENT DEVELOPMENT STAFF 2000

Chapter 12

Twelve Days of Darkness

Surprisingly, I slept well that night, probably from sheer exhaustion, and the next night, as well. I woke up on Tuesday morning with an eerie sense of comfort. I never knew how much prayer could work until I faced the death of a best friend in 1996; and now four years later, I faced this huge emotional setback again. We knew there were literally hundreds of people praying sincerely and deeply for our pain. I can think of no greater confirmation of the phrase "Peace that passes all understanding" than the way I felt during this severe crisis.

It almost makes you wish everyone could go through something similar to experience the tangible nature of their faith in God. By the middle of the morning, I was so joyful again, I wondered if I were dealing with the issue at all. The Lord seemed to be carrying almost the entire burden to make sure I could get through the process. What a great God we have!

Angie and I spent the rest of the day caring for each other and doing little things around the house. As the news spread, friends began to drop by. Some apologized for intruding, but felt they could not rest until they had expressed their sorrow and love. Others simply offered a hug, a prayer, or some food, and then quickly moved on to allow us to grieve in private.

The first person to demonstrate real anger was my nephew, Austin, age 5. He told his mother he wanted to spit on the birthmother. The innocence of a child can often cut through normal social manners with a brutally honest gut response, and he expressed the intensity of emotion that my brother's children felt on my behalf. I appreciated his empathy, even if I didn't concur with his suggested response, and knew that he wouldn't actually do such a thing, either.

Of course I didn't want to spit on anyone, and certainly not on Milli. I wanted to hug her and counsel her through this catastrophic moment in her life. She needed to know that we all loved her and cared for her and wanted what was best for her. She needed to feel God's presence and guidance through whatever lay ahead in her time of anguish and confusion, even if it emotionally dragged us under the bus.

Dr. Jerry Cain, President of Judson College, stopped by and with tears streaming prayed for us, and told me to take as long as I needed away from the office. My staff and my peers called and requested my workload so they could handle any responsibilities that needed immediate attention. Friends offered to mow the lawn, wash our car, and bring us food. We accepted the food, but tried to do some of the basic household chores ourselves to work off the despondency.

Our first trip away from home in four days was to visit our pastor and his wife. They offered the right mixture of sadness, anger, hope, and understanding for us to know we were in good spiritual hands. Joyce, the pastor's wife, was the first person to state publicly and in our presence that she thought the birth-mother would change her mind and call us after the shock was over and the reality of raising twin boys set in.

This was a bold declaration and Joyce is not a woman prone to fantasy or plastic Christian communication. This was not an "it will make them feel better" offhand comment to lighten the emotional pain that she couldn't bear. This is a tough, authentic, seasoned saint. She was speaking from her heart and what she believed God had revealed to her. As much as we didn't want to totally grab hope yet again so soon, her words really encouraged us to have faith that God would act somehow, someway!

Outside of visiting Tim and Joyce, we requested the company of only one person outside of our immediate family, and that was the president's secretary, Jill Malohn. As the days started to pass and the pain started to settle, I knew we needed some significant depth of empathy. Jill had confided in me previously that she had lost three children to death: one in a drowning accident at age three, one in an auto accident when Jill was eight months pregnant, and one that was stillborn. She certainly understood grieving and she already had bonded with us after she had learned of our nine-year waiting game. We had developed a strong mother-son type of relationship in the administrative circle, and with my mom and Angie's mom hundreds of miles away, Jill was the mother of choice to console us.

Besides, Jill's family story was not all just tragedies. She and her husband had persevered and adopted two children in an era when it was less accepted. Those who know Jill, but don't know her story, find it hard to believe that such a joyful, giving, and caring woman could have gone through such profound agony and despair. This was the friend I wanted to hold my wife during her trauma. This was the woman who could share with Angie how to make it through another day, another week, another month, and get on with life through the coming years.

Jill and Angie spent some time together that was deeply spiritual. Unlike men of wisdom and faith who, in a time like this, usually fill the air with quotes from great books and stories of heroes Jill simply opened her soul and allowed the memories of her pain to be available to Angie's pain. The two of them touched each other's hearts in ways that only women can. Jill offered no specific plan, no pat answers, and no easy path to recovery. What she offered my wife was who she is, what she had been through, and where it had taken her. We are grateful for her love and kindness.

As the week went on and the magnitude of the failed placement took hold, I found myself yearning for some method of expressing myself besides conversation and tears. We had set up an appointment with Becky and told her during the session to leave our name on the profile list. Though we had wanted to dramatically remove ourselves from the list as a response to the pain, the only people it would have hurt were us! Becky had done a nice job gently nudging us in that direction anyway, and though we didn't really feel it yet, we knew it was the wisest way to tangibly return to life. Oh, how years of my own counseling experiences came rummaging through my soul in a whole new way. I would never underestimate again anybody's pain and the emotional responses and behavior that can result from it.

I wrote a letter to Milli that Angie and I had worked on as we tried to bring closure to the failed placement. We asked Becky at the meeting if it would be appropriate to send the letter to her. After making sure that we were not planning some kind of emotional retaliatory strike, Becky asked us to send the letter through Sunny Ridge so she could give it to Milli and avoid any confusion.

Writing the letter to Milli gave me a much-needed cathartic release. We still have the letter because Becky returned it to us because she never had the opportunity to send it. Since the writing had been so beneficial to my spirit, the next day I wrote a poem called "Denied."

While creating the poem, late at night and by myself, I grieved in the inner chambers of my heart for the first time. The intensity of the tears scared me, but it felt really good at the same time. I put a copy of the poem on our kitchen refrigerator door, and let Angie read it on her own time. A day later I snuck over to Judson really early in the morning to avoid seeing anybody, and displayed the poem on my office door. Being a gregarious and self-disclosing leader, I needed my friends and colleagues to see and feel the depths of my anguish, though I wasn't quite ready to see them face to face.

I include the poem here. You can see that I start the poem in a whimsical manner, mocking myself for believing a trivial incident, like a message in a fortune cookie, might be confirmation of God's plan in our lives. As the poem continues you can feel my frustration and sadness build. The emotional release and healing followed the same progression.

DENIED

Are fortune cookies credible besides being edible?
Is God's plan as painful as the hole in my soul?
What do we do now in the quest to fill our quiver?
How long will this yearning to parent be denied?

I don't doubt the truth of my Savior's sovereignty,
But why must I hurt so much for His goal?
I think it's easier with answers that are monthly,
Than to grab on to hope for a four-month ride.
I don't want to be known as the couple without,

Or the first on the prayer list as we continue to mourn.
Is there any satisfaction or honor for being considered
The best choice to parent our friends' kids if they die?

A nursery room full of promise and of unmet desires.
Sixty-three stars and a bright yellow moon.
Two Winnie the Pooh's sit alone in a rocker,
No one to bite them and cover them with drool.

Two car seats, two bouncies, two hearts that are broken.
Too much love and attention with nowhere to go.
No more tears are necessary to induce my sorrow,
No comforting words do I offer as we cry.

They were born on the 17th of June, in the evening,
The same day we were married, back in '89.
One last confirmation that now is so hollow.
How long will this yearning to parent be denied?

Writing the poem helped me finally begin to work through the pain, so I decided to write a magazine article for other couples who had experienced a failed placement. Earlier when I'd mentioned the idea to Becky, she had encouraged me and said she didn't know of any such article in the current adoption literature, wisely recognizing that I needed that outlet.

The next night I went to the computer again around midnight.

Crying as I worked, I wrote the article in one sitting. Fashioning my sadness into the concept and language of a magazine article brought the joy of serving others to my grieving process. As an educator and counselor, I confirmed firsthand, internally, what I had often told my students and clients: the act of giving and sharing will heal a wounded soul.

I sent a copy of the article to Sunny Ridge, then emailed a copy to *Adoptive Families* magazine. Shortly thereafter, publisher Susan Caughman responded with a request to include the article in an upcoming issue. The article appeared in the May/June, 2001, issue of the magazine, as follows.

COPING WITH A FAILED ADOPTION
Tips for keeping the dream of a child alive
after a crushing disappointment.

A week ago our placement failed. My wife, Angie, and I will remember forever—the birthmother's delivery date was our wedding anniversary. However, amidst this emotional anguish, we offer these suggestions to help you get past the pain.

1. Allow your friends to help you. Most of us love to serve others in their time of need but feel that we are "putting someone out" if they want to return the favor. But, do yourself and your family a tremendous favor—accept the help!

Welcome the hugs, the tears, the prayers, the food, the work relief, the babysitting offers, and, if warranted, the monetary aid. As your friends begin to call you and the neighbors visit, think about your needs so your support group can put their love to work. Nobody knows what to say when these types of incidents occur. Give your loved ones something useful, practical, and helpful to do instead.

2. Let your partner grieve in his or her own way. Some men believe it is a sign of strength to go back to the grind immediately after loss. But you don't care for your wife by leaving her alone to grieve; you show withdrawal and insensitivity. So tell your colleagues at work to cover your meetings; ask your golf buddy to mow your lawn.

As for you, just be with your wife. Don't talk unless spoken to, don't caress unless she asks you to, and don't have the TV on in the background. Your presence will convey your commitment and your silence will honor her loss.

Though your husband may not break down in tears five times a day, don't underestimate his pain. Do not expect him to embrace his male friends and collapse into sobs. It may happen, but it is not likely. Let the housework go for a week, or more. Know which of your friends will listen and hold you and which ones will, unfortunately, want to solve your problem. Seek out women who have been through miscarriages or infant deaths, or other couples who have failed placements. Their wisdom will be invaluable to you as you try to imagine your future.

3. Seek closure. Examine what you have really lost and what you still need to move forward. Some couples box up the toys, put away the stroller, and repaint the baby room immediately. Others make minor alterations and prepare for the next go around. There's no right or wrong answer, but an impulsive, spur-of-the-moment reaction is not the one to follow.

Throwing the car seat in the river and the stuffed animals in the fireplace may release some pent-up anger and feel wickedly satisfying for the moment, but you will probably regret it later. Discuss it as a couple or with a few cherished friends, and come up with a plan.

Write letters to the birthmother, God, or your agency. Let them sit, and if after a week the letters still seem appropriate, send them. Express yourself in ways that are your normal creative outlets: write music or poetry, make a symbolic craft or a video. Your emotions will often sneak into the endeavor and bring spontaneous healing moments that otherwise may be missed.

4. Make peace with God. Almost anyone who has considered adoption has considered God to be a part of the equation. When you face infertility or loss, the acknowledgment of a higher power is inevitable. The inability to control our environment and, consequently, our circumstances leads us to the ultimate question: is there a God? And if so, why would He allow this to happen? He is ever identified as one or not. If, like me, you believe that God is sovereign, why hold back your feelings? He's aware of them.

It's a mistake to think that these suggestions will bring instantaneous and complete relief. Only time will do that. But your approach to grieving can determine whether you're going to be deeply depressed or extremely sad, despondent and bitter or disappointed and frustrated, fearful and doubting or able to trust again. Most importantly, will you be able to dream of a child and re-risk the rejection, the failure, the heartache?

Thanks to the support of God, our family, friends, and our adoption agency, we began our search for a child to adopt anew yesterday.

The article generated a huge response. My mother and several friends passed copies of the magazine to friends and loved ones who had suffered similar placement failures. It was truly uplifting to know that our pain and grieving process helped others to work through their loss and grieving. But, none of it changed the fact that I still wasn't a dad.

PLACEMENT DAY AT SUNNY RIDGE

ELIAH AND JACOB

CHAPTER 13

Placement Day!

About a week after the failed placement, we received a phone call from Susan Weber, our campus nurse at Judson. She and her husband, Laverne, offered us their vacation home in Lake Geneva, Wisconsin, for a few days of grieving, recuperation, and readjustment of our family dreams. We gladly accepted. After spending some time with the Webers to get instructions and directions, we departed for the northern air and some respite on a Sunday night, the 25th of June.

Their beautiful lake home is located three-quarters of a mile away from the shore on the southwest side of Lake Geneva. We took advantage of the atmosphere of the surrounding community and also were the benefactors of some mild summer temperatures. This allowed us to take long walks at both dawn and dusk each day where we appreciated the marvelous homes, the impressive docks, and the expansive gardens. Getting away from the pain of our empty home did help us breathe again.

In between the fresh clean air and the exercise, we spent hours near each other, but often remained in complete silence. I did some Bible research, especially in Job, and worked on concepts for our Student Development department at the college. Angie cut coupons and read back issues of *Good Housekeeping* and *Country Living*. We went out for a drive, too, once a day, and took in a different restaurant each night for dinner. After dark we enjoyed the programs that were on the television from three different PBS stations, one from Milwaukee and two from Chicago. Several of them were about overcoming hardship and suffering. We absorbed them without verbal reflection.

By Wednesday June 28th, we began to talk about our parenting future and once again speculated on what might develop. We also talked of what might have been as we recycled and buried the visions we had seen so vividly in our minds, visions of twin boys scampering around the house babbling to their mother in the kitchen and playing ball with me in the back yard.

In my classes on premarital and early marital studies, I had learned about the different ways couples will secure and develop intimacy levels that sustain and stabilize a marriage. This moment in our lives was a difficult event, to be sure. It was up to us to use this time and this opportunity, painful though it may be, to strengthen our marriage.

Crisis intimacy is always one of the most important intimacy styles necessary for a strong marriage. Couples who respond affectionately and compassionately to each other in crisis can usually survive in other areas of intimacy such as intellectual, creative, financial, sexual, and social intimacy.

I'm thankful that Angie and I, despite our often combative communication patterns, have always handled crises in a way that has resulted in a stronger bond of love. This current crisis was certainly the most profound eruption of chaos in our eleven years of marriage. And our love for each other was once again moving into deeper levels that probably couldn't have been reached without pain and loss.

Thursday morning, the 29th of June, was our last full day scheduled at the Webers' home. At about 10:00 AM, as I was finishing my study of the book of Job at the kitchen table, the phone rang. It was only the second call we had received all week. It was Tory and Sandy Gum, our good friends from Judson. They invited us to see their new home off Lake Como, another beautiful lakeside community a few miles northwest of Lake Geneva. Tory was the women's basketball coach at Judson, so we had coached together for a few years and his office was right next to mine in Student Development. Sandy and Angie had both been Resident Directors for three years and had also spent much time together.

At the time, Tory and Sandy were expecting their fourth child and conceptions had not been difficult. The last two times they had become pregnant Tory had come and shared with me in private before I heard the news through the public grapevine. Friends with the sensitivity to think of how their joyful news might be difficult for others to process are the kind of people you want to stay involved with for life.

So, for the first time in almost two weeks, Angie and I looked forward to being with friends again. We consider the Gums to be part of our extended family anyway, and they were the perfect people to hang out with as we eased our way back into the normal world. They both could be fun and serious and knew us well enough not to worry about either extreme. Tory gave me directions to his home and we told them we would see them in about an hour.

About fifteen minutes later the phone rang again. I leisurely reached for the receiver expecting to hear Tory's voice with a correction or clarification on getting to his place. Instead, it was our caseworker, Becky, and the energy in her voice was electrifying. She told me I'd better sit down. I stumbled back a few feet, found a chair, and said, "OK, I'm ready."

Her first question was quick and to the point and with unmasked joy. "Would you still be interested in parenting twins?" I was still adjusting to not hearing Tory's voice, but I managed to speak.

"Absolutely," I said, with as much confidence as I could muster in a state of shock! Physically, I was not quite as confident. My stomach churned immediately, my head spun, and a cold sweat broke out all over my body! Becky went on to inform me that

Milli had spent several days isolated in a hotel room without the boys trying to come to a resolution about the lack of peace she felt about her change of heart. She concluded that she would not try to raise the boys herself, and she was ready to go through with the placement. Most importantly, that placement was still with us!

And not only was she ready and determined, but she wanted to do it as soon as possible. Like, now! When Becky asked how soon we could get to the agency office at Wheaton, I asked first, out of a natural fearful reaction, for a confirmation of their arrival (Milli and the twins) before we drove all that way from Lake Geneva, Wisconsin, back to Wheaton, Illinois. Then, just like the original selection call on April 3rd, I asked Becky to repeat to Angie the entire scenario she had just told me and handed the phone to my shocked and pale wife who had overheard much of the conversation.

As Becky and Angie talked about the happenings of the last several days, I paced around the house like a caged animal. I couldn't control my excitement, my fear, my emotions, my energy, or my nerves, so I grabbed the vacuum cleaner, headed down-stairs, and began to clean the house. It was either that or run down to the lake and back, but I figured Angie would want to talk when she hung up the phone and would be a bit confused, and angry, if I wasn't in the house.

After Angie put the receiver down we hugged and cried and prayed together for wisdom and emotional strength, and then

Angie called Milli to finalize the plans. They talked together like old friends who hadn't kept in contact, but could slip back into familiar roles and patterns with ease. Though it was not necessary, I heard the women share unconditional responses of forgiveness and acceptance. That gave me a little more peace in moving forward.

The final agreement was this: we agreed that we would drive back to Elgin, but would not go to Wheaton until Milli and the boys arrived first. We wanted some kind of leverage before we allowed our hearts to be on the line again. As soon as Angie was done talking to Milli, she went to the bathroom and vomited. It was now about 11:00 AM.

The next twelve hours will be emotionally and visually cemented in my memory forever. After cleaning the house, we took the fifteen-minute drive to Lake Como, surprised the Gums with our incredible news, and then hustled back to Elgin. Once home, we changed clothes, gathered our belongings, gave the house a brief once over, called our pastor for prayer, threw the unopened car seat boxes in the back of our car, and waited for the call from Wheaton. It was about 5:00 PM when Becky called. They wanted us to be there in thirty minutes.

We had decided immediately after leaving Wisconsin not to call our families until the papers were signed. We didn't want them to get filled with hope again without any complete assurance that the placement would go through this time. The risk of two broken hearts seemed worth it, but not nine or ten all over the

Midwest. We knew the twelve days had been devastating to our parents, siblings, and many of our friends, as well.

We arrived at Sunny Ridge a half hour late due to traffic, and were quickly whisked away to a different caseworker's office. Matt and Milli and the boys were a mere twenty feet from us finishing their paper work. They were so close, but still seemed so far away.

The energy was alive in the building! It was obvious to us that every staff member there knew what was going down and was pretty excited. Arlene, who had started this whole process with the phone message nearly a year ago, was now the one walking us through the paperwork. I fully admit that we signed mindlessly without the careful reading we usually would have given such documents. At this point, we would have signed away our fingers and toes to complete the placement forms. I would have chopped one or two off right then and there if that is what it would have taken to secure the deal.

When we were done, we still had to wait for a while. One last waiting period! During those twenty minutes we asked Arlene a hundred nervous questions and she graciously answered every one with joy. What an amazing role the adoption caseworkers play. Conduits and exchange agents of dreams and fulfillment. It must be a job of a thousand emotions.

Around 6:30 PM, after Becky and Arlene had thoroughly analyzed all documents for completion, Arlene took us down the hall and into Becky's office where Milli and Matt and the boys were waiting. They were waiting for us and our wait to parent was finally over. Only entering the gates of heaven some day will be able to top that entry.

When we entered the room, the four of them were sitting directly in our visual line so there was no wasted searching. Milli was holding Jacob and Matt was holding Eliah. They were seated very close together on a couch and seemed almost huddled and protective. Becky sat in a chair that was adjacent to the couch and Milli's sister Mindi was in a second chair across from Becky's. There were two other chairs, empty, directly across from our future.

Angie took the lead for us, immediately and enthusiastically pronouncing the boys to be "beautiful . . . just beautiful." I had no idea what to say about the precious little dark-haired, dark-eyed bundles. I was completely removed from my emotions. I couldn't process anything. I just stared at those two little living creatures, trying to envision them coming home with me. It felt like an out-of-body experience. I fumbled with my words awkwardly and commented on, of all things, their outfits. I didn't care about their clothes! I just had absolutely no idea how to communicate the intensity of my feelings. I wondered if I looked as desperately weak and frail as I felt.

Milli graciously asked us if we wanted to hold them and thankfully Angie was in the room to say "yes." I'm not sure what I would have uttered next, maybe something about their socks, so I was thankful I had a partner in the room. What took place next is ingrained in my hard drive forever.

There is something remarkably profound about a birthmother handing her child to an adoptive mother, and in this case, it was doubled, as the birthfather handed me a child, as well. I almost couldn't take the exchange. After all the years and all the pain, my time of fulfillment had arrived and I was dumbfounded and weak kneed. Where was my normal composure and strength under pressure?

That handoff of our boys is the most amazing gesture and the most selfless gift of unconditional love outside of the death of Jesus on the cross that will ever be available to me. These two young adults were handing us their most precious possession, the very creation of their two bodies and souls, and they trusted us to fulfill their hopes and dreams for them. Talk about sacrifice! Could I have done the same? Could I do it now?

I can think of nothing more Christ-like than for a couple to give their flesh and blood to another couple, relinquishing all rights and privileges in an effort to secure the best possible future for their beloved. I felt humbled and unworthy of this gift. I gingerly nestled Eliah in the crook of my arm, afraid to look up at Matt for a reaction and staring at Angie for any non-verbal or verbal cues of inappropriate or improper baby handling. I was completely out of any element of experience or skill and prayed that all of them would forgive me when Eliah began to have convulsions or gag because of the way I was holding him.

We took pictures and then listened intently as Milli told us the boys' habits, their likes, their schedule, and their differences and frustrations. Of course, I can't remember one word of that exchange! Angie changed Jacob's diaper like a veteran, and gently gave me directions for handling and positioning Eliah for the first of many ten-minute ordeals.

Then, after another twenty minutes of casual and reserved conversation, Milli announced that she was ready to leave. She asked me to follow her to the car to get some of the boys' clothes. She was so confident and at peace. So poised and in control. It felt like she was the experienced counselor and I was the young adult.

Matt and Milli each kissed both of the boys again, and Becky asked me to close with a prayer. I am glad she asked me this at the end of the gathering and not the beginning or it might have been the most awkward moment of sustained silence in the history of their agency. Thankfully, by that time I had gained enough sense of reality and enough composure to give an appropriate blessing.

After putting their belongings in the trunk of my car, I hugged Milli good-bye and shook Matt's hand with the most warmth I could offer. I am a serious hugger, but I had no idea about Matt's hugging preferences, so I didn't offer that kind of move at this juncture. I reminded them that I would send pictures and letters, but Matt told me he wasn't sure he was ready for any of that. I said OK, but if he would let me know when he was ready, I would be happy to oblige. Then, they got in their car and drove out of the parking lot, leaving their sons with us! What a strange and fascinating moment that was. I felt ashamedly vindicated. But as strange and bewildered as I felt, I wondered how heart wrenching and painful that must have been for them.

After a frozen moment in the parking lot, I finished loading all of the gear and belongings into the car, slammed the door, and sprinted back to the main building. Now, I was getting super excited and I wanted to hold my beloved sons again. I yanked on the front door and nearly pulled my shoulder out of its socket. It was locked! Angie had come to her senses and had ordered the agency on lockdown. I rang the door bell and tried to ignore the bizarre and ridiculous scenarios that were running through my head once again. When would I return to my normal state of chaotic psychosis? This new level was even scary to me!

MILLI AND BOYS 2001

CHAPTER 14

Two for the Show

When I got back into the office with Becky, Angie, and the boys, the magnitude of what we were involved in and the enormous emotions of the day began to surface. I couldn't stop smiling, but I felt queasy and terrified that something would still go wrong, something that we hadn't planned on or couldn't foresee.

After talking with Becky about some basics in childcare, we immediately asked her to take us through the timing and schedule of all of the court dates and legal documents. In hindsight, although I am sure this is common, the timing might have looked insensitive and cold, but we just couldn't help ourselves. Our trust factor was low, and our hearts were not fully recovered yet, even with the boys in our immediate possession.

After being reassured several times, we finally called both families to report the news. We started with my brother Warren and his wife Lea so they could serve as the communications headquarters. It was nice to shock everyone with good news, for a change. As our family members expressed their joy and relief, my joy was building. The more relatives I talked with, the more confident I felt. Soon I was in one of my manic highs. We were now the parents of two beautiful baby boys! I was finally a dad! Angie was finally a mom! We were finally parents!

We hugged every employee in the building and then headed for the car and the start of our future. The future had finally come! The future was finally here!

After figuring out how to strap the baby chairs in our car's second-row bucket seats (a process that has brought many a man to tears or cursing—do they think women are the only ones who have to put their hands through the 2" plastic seatbelt tunnel in the back of those things?!?), we put the boys in place for safe travel and set off down the road to our dreams.

Immediately, I began to drive like the people I've always criticized. You know the ones I am talking about. The guys that go ten miles below the speed limit, put their turn signals on a mile before they're going to turn, and tap their brakes fifty feet away from an approaching green light, just in case it should turn yellow, let alone red. I kept looking in the rearview mirror to make sure the boys were still OK, beginning a whole new era in my life, an era of caution, protection, and concern. Had I turned into a real dad that quickly? Had I just aged ten years?

When we pulled into our driveway around 8:30 PM, my brother and his family were waiting with honks, cheers, hugs, and celebration. We called the remaining of our closest friends, who passed the word around to the rest of Elgin, Ohio, and Iowa for us. Where was WGN—the Chicago Super Station? Didn't they know we were home?

A steady stream of loved ones filed through the house until we feared for the boys' bodies and I had eaten all the remaining snacks in the cupboards. Those two sweet bundles of love had been snuggled and kissed a hundred times, and although they weren't fussing, we worried that all the handling would make for a long tomorrow morning. We were right. It did.

After two whirlwind days of over forty visitors and countless gifts and warm embraces, we were just plain exhausted. Eliah and Jacob were not sleeping at night, and we were still working through all the newborn baby issues like nipple preference, successful burping techniques, and the meaning of different crying sounds from the physically identical, but emotionally different baby boys.

Furthermore, I had done no babysitting in my teen years and had refused to change diapers for any of my friends' or even my brother's children. This meant I was in an accelerated and advanced baby care program, with no time for trial and error. I put aside my pride and my will, and I gladly took orders from Angie and all other mothers who offered tips and suggestions on all aspects of baby care.

I believe it was July 1st when once again our "baby angel,"

the new name I had given Nurse Weber, called to ask if she could come over for a quick visit. Despite our fatigue, we welcomed her enthusiastically. After the appropriate cuddles and snuggles were delivered, Susan took a book out of her purse and offered it to me. The book she had brought for us was *Baby Wise*, by Gary and Anne Marie Ezzo. The book turned out to be exactly what Angie and I needed to give us confidence that our inclination toward a parent-based, structured style of child rearing was the right style and technique for us. Susan once again played an important role in our family future.

The principle of this small and simple book is that parents must create schedules of sleep, feeding, and play time that fit into their own needs and give regularity and predictability to the babies' lives. This system is especially beneficial for parents of multiples and if done with consistency brings structure to the family.

By nature, Angie is so highly organized and structured that she wore this system of child rearing like an old t-shirt in no time at all. I am, by nature, not this way, and it definitely took me a while to get in the swing of it. Within a couple of months, though, she had all her boys (me included) settled into a comfortable and dependable routine that really worked for us.

The rest of our first summer as parents flew by with the regularity of our new patterns and roles. I'm glad our first experience with babies was twins. It forced me to be completely involved 100% of the time. When Eliah was hungry at 2 AM, so was Jacob.

When Jacob needed a diaper change, Eliah probably did, too; if not right away, a short time later. Angie and I often traded two-hour naps with baby care duties. We were both sleep-deprived for the first five months—nothing new for new parents!

Whatever it took, Angie was there on the job. No complaint. No hesitation. And except for an occasional visit by grandparents who took over certain duties, I tried to be there the same way. It was difficult, and the routine really challenged my random nature, but I survived and even enjoyed it. I think the time without children helped me appreciate even the mundane aspects of child rearing, at least initially!

Soon, however, the summer was over and I reluctantly went back into my role as a college administrator. While there, I would often pause at my desk to reflect on the events of the last six months. It was all so consuming and often I couldn't gain any perspective until I was at work and away from the environment. Since the day we came home with the boys, Angie and I had not really had a single moment to ourselves. We were always on the brink of exhaustion and we were still on an emotional roller coaster. What we needed was a weekend to get away, and to communicate about our past six months. We began to make plans for something in late September or early October.

That chance never came, though. The roller coaster was about to skip the home docking station and head right back up the beginning mountain for another long and frenetic ride. Life was telling us to put our safety harness on and to keep our hands and feet securely inside of the car. It was really about to get interesting!

IV. THE BIOLOGICAL SURPRISE

KEVIN AND VICKI RAHN AND JACOB

ANGIE AND VICKI AND THE BOYS

CHAPTER 15

Labor Day

A very strange thing happened in August, and it wasn't just a departure from our normal crazy schedule! August is always the busiest month for someone working in higher education, and this particular August of 2000, we had some additional distractions.

First, the summer sports camp rotation had scheduled my two youth basketball camps during the last week of July and the first week of August. These were weeks of great fun and good money, but they were very long and tiring days! Secondly, we had several family members and friends living with us, and had to host a 25-person Japanese basketball team on campus with daily sightseeing trips all over Chicagoland. This was on top of administrating all of the student activities that initiate the beginning of school! See what I mean about August being busy?

No, what was strange this particular August was that for the first time in our eleven-year marriage Angie was late with her cycle! At first we dismissed it as a reaction to the stress and strain of all those chaotic activities. After a week or so, though, we went into full denial, and ignored any conversation resembling the topic. Eventually, Angie counted and recounted her days and convinced herself that she was really off by a week in her memory.

Finally, on Labor Day, after we had finished the late-night feeding, and knowing that Angie was at a minimum at least two weeks late, I looked her dead in the eye, and blurted out, "You're pregnant!"

"There's no way," she said. "I can't be." As always, in times of debate and intensity, she was persuasive in her defense and I mentally backed down a bit. This was despite the fact that her chiropractor verbally had suspected the same, unbeknownst to me, just a few days before.

"Prove it," I said, and she couldn't hide a slight smile. This was all I needed to see to then coax and cajole her into running to the drug store for a home pregnancy test, though it was after midnight!

As I waited for her return, I paced around the house talking to myself, to God, to our boys asleep in their bedroom, and to our future. Despite my apprehension with the possible results, it was very exciting, primarily because she never had had a reason to take a pregnancy test before. This was another wonderful first in our busy summer of new beginnings. By the time Angie came back I could tell that she had also been mentally eroding her internal wall of denial.

She bolted up the back porch stairs, burst through the kitchen door, and flush with excitement scampered into the bathroom. Her reaction then triggered apprehension in me. As I munched on my third bowl of cereal, I began to wonder what would happen if indeed she were pregnant. After a decade of infertility, and then the yearlong adoption procedures, could we possibly be pregnant now, when we didn't really want or need to be? And if we were, what in the world were we going to do? How could we take care of another baby? Suddenly, my soggy Golden Grahams™ weren't very tasty.

"Uh huh! Uh huh!" Angie was sending some kind of guttural signal from her soul. I raced into the bathroom to look at the little strip. It was purple, the royal sign of a positive test. We locked eyes, but were too shocked to react in any immediate manner. We stared at the strip, then at each other, and then back at the strip.

Our first spontaneous emotion was laughter. We laughed and hugged and began to talk to God out loud about his sense of humor. We danced around in the bathroom like we had won the lottery, but weren't 100% sure our ticket was valid, and weren't sure what to do to claim the jackpot! We initially decided to keep the news to ourselves until an obstetrician could confirm the pregnancy. That didn't last long.

After twenty minutes we decided to tell our families right away, even though it was now after 2:00 in Cincinnati! We wanted everyone to enjoy this ironic turn of events with us and we couldn't wait to share the crazy news. After all, they had been cheering for us for so many years that we wanted them to know right away. Our normal sleep-deprived night of feedings extended into a sleepless night of shock and amazement.

Whenever we told anyone, their immediate reaction was usually laughter. Sometimes, they broke right down in hysterics. And everyone seemed to know another married couple who went through the same experience right after adoption. Then when the giggles stopped, they almost always shifted to concern and questions about how we would survive with three babies under a year old. They were on the same mental adjustment we were.

As a reaction to this epic event, even prior to passing the first trimester, we made several significant and major life changes. First, I resigned from my job as head coach of the Judson men's basketball team. I had planned to do this in the near future, but I had anticipated coaching for about four more years. That was the amount of time I felt I needed in order to establish a winning program. Our team was just starting to gain some firm foundations for success. Now, I had to let go of that dream and that goal. This was very difficult to do for a driven achiever, and that was without even thinking about the feelings of the players.

Telling the guys turned out to be one of the hardest things I've ever done professionally. We'd had a really strong finish to the season the previous year, winning five of our last seven games, including our first conference playoff game, and we had lost only one of the starting five players to graduation. There were also several strong recruits who had just signed on to play for me for four years! We were on the edge of a very promising year. Several days earlier I had met with several of the upper classmen to lay out the structure for the upcoming season. How a few days can change your world!

I opened the meeting with the overused cliché, "I have some good news and some bad news." And then I went straight to the point: "Angie and I are pregnant." They laughed and cheered. I am a very open person and the coach/player relationship is an intimate one, so they all knew my family circumstances. "The bad news is that I am resigning as basketball coach of Judson College, effective immediately."

Complete silence. Blank stares at the floor. "Assistant Coach Doug Lee will now take over as interim coach," I continued. Then after a few more minutes of nothing, I opened the floor for comments and questions. The team captain said how happy he was for us. Several more similar comments were made. There were only a few questions, and I was honored because none of them had to do with basketball. They asked when Angie was due. When did we learn she was pregnant? Did we want another set of twins? There were several other inquiries, some pertinent and some humorous. Then I told them it was time for me to put Coach Lee in charge and to go home to put my boys to bed. My team was now at home.

I prayed for all of us and the emotions started building through the prayer.

When I finished, I just walked slowly down the middle of the room and out the back door. I couldn't look at them, but I think they understood. They even clapped for me. I've had a lot of applause in my career as an athlete and musician, but I've never been as touched by spontaneous appreciation as I was at that moment. I left the gym, sat down on a bench outside the entrance door, and cried for twenty minutes. It was bittersweet that I had to give up the winning-coach dream to actualize my winning-parent dream, but some losses are even joyful.

I stayed in a contemplative mood as I returned to my car and drove off the campus. It was only a five-minute ride to my house. As odd as it may sound for a sports junkie who was living out a dream to coach at his alma mater, by the time I arrived home, I had put my coaching days behind me and had placed fathering at the center of my new priorities. It was the right decision and I had complete peace. God was already healing and adjusting my drive and focus.

The second major life change was in our living arrangement. Our Victorian home had actually been built as a two-unit dwelling. Angie and I were currently living downstairs. A married professional couple lived upstairs. They had been there twelve years and were ideal tenants. Despite being the owners, we often felt that we lived in their house due to their long tenure.

But now, in light of our growing family, we had to ask the house doctors, as we called them, Dr. Scott and Dr. Claire, to leave. Not because we needed the living space for ourselves yet, but because we needed to find someone who could provide child-care assistance for Angie. We did not see a way of handling all of the additional issues without some significant help.

After several months of praying, searching, and considering different couples, in November, Kevin and Vicki Rahn agreed to become our involved tenants. Drs Scott and Claire teased us that we had evicted them, but they found a condo close by in the area and scheduled a moving date near Christmas. I think the forced move was actually good for them also.

Kevin and Vicki broke their lease and planned on moving in with us in late January. That gave me a month to replace some carpet and to paint all of the rooms. I had known Kevin and his brothers, Bill and Brian, for several years—as students, as basket-ball players on Judson teams, and as hardworking farm boys with solid Christian values. Kevin's wife, Vicki, took over right away as our nanny. Vicki had done some educational tutoring with my nephew Austin, and we had been very impressed with her nur-turing and mothering skills. She was a straight-A student with a huge heart for children. We looked forward to the help and to the camaraderie. What an enormous blessing they would be to us.

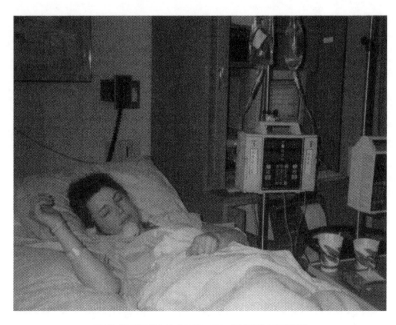

ANGIE IN BIRTHING ROOM, ST. ALEXIUS HOSPITAL

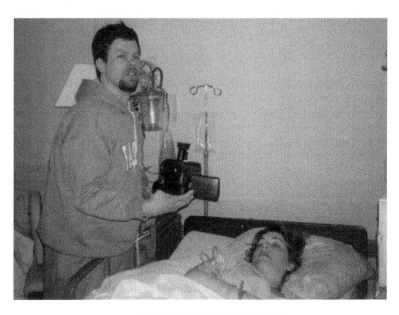

WAITING TO GET A PICTURE OF ALIVIA

CHAPTER 16

Check-Up and Check-In

On Monday morning, March 19, 2001, Angie and I went to the North Suburban Clinic to see our midwife, Patty Fornoff. Patty had assisted Sandy Gum in delivering a couple of their babies, and Sandy assured us that we would be in good hands. She was right. We liked Patty the moment we met.

We also hired Nurse Weber to be our "Doula," a Greek term for a birthing helper. Susan's role was to assist Patty as she attended to Angie's physical and emotional needs, and in our case, to keep me from getting in the way. We were prepared and ready for the last two months of the pregnancy, hopeful that Angie would have a normal delivery. Unfortunately, that was not to occur—not even close!

At the six-month check-up, Patty had cautioned Angie that her blood pressure was a little high and that her feet were too swollen. Nothing that serious, but we were to be observant. Now, at the seventh month, those same conditions were getting out of control, and Patty's whole approach turned minute-by-minute to a very grim concern. Angie's blood pressure was now sky high, her feet were swollen out of her normal shoes, and her skin was getting a strange, unhealthy look and color.

If that were not enough, Angie's urinalysis revealed a critically high level of protein, meaning, we learned later, that her kidneys were not functioning well. Patty went into high gear now, and she bolted out of the examining room to confer with Angie's doctor.

She returned shortly and informed us that she needed another ultrasound as soon as possible. Her look of concern had not diminished, but she did say that we could go home for now. She requested that we schedule an appointment as soon as possible and demanded that we get Angie off her feet for the duration of the pregnancy. She promised that she would call us as soon as she looked at the results of the protein test. The growing nausea in my stomach gained intensity.

This was actually the second time we had been ordered to have an additional ultrasound. The first came in the third month when Angie's doctors were concerned that she had placenta previa, a condition where the placenta is lying on top or partially blocking the cervix. That problem had subsided enough that it was not a concern now, although hindsight would suggest that it might have had something to do with the ultimate diagnosis.

On our way out of the office, we stopped at the front desk to schedule the extra test but had difficulty finding a time that worked for Angie, Vicki, and me. It looked as if we would have to wait until Thursday, the 22nd of March, three days away. Not too bad, but not good enough for this concerned husband and father. While we were discussing possible times and holding up the line, the office manager received a phone call resulting in a cancellation and offered that spot to us. Once again, God put his stamp on this baby and my wife, as we were able to have the ultrasound at 1:00 PM that very afternoon! As it turned out, the 22nd would have been too late and could have cost me one or both of the precious ladies currently in my life!

As we left the clinic to go grab a quick lunch (nausea usually does not stop me from eating), I stopped to make a phone call to Terri Acres, our Student Development office manager. I had the distinct feeling that I would not be returning to work for quite a while. It turned out to be a very long while.

Angie and I went to Taco Bell and then stopped for a short time at Babies R Us to kill some time. Stubborn as always, Angie was still not staying off her feet. As 1:00 PM approached, we ventured back to the clinic for the additional ultrasound. Neither of us spoke much about this new and obviously dangerous development in Angie's pregnancy. We just didn't have enough real information to discuss the issue or enough energy to even try.

By this time, we were quite familiar with ultrasound procedures, so when the attendant took an extra long look at certain areas, and answered Angie's nervous questions abruptly and without explanation, we knew there was trouble. After the hour long exam (twice as long as our normal visits), we returned to a patient room to wait for Patty. She arrived shortly thereafter. In a firm and matter-of-fact tone, Patty said that Angie had to see an obstetrician without delay, and then she left without any hint, explanation, or alternative options.

As it so happened, Angie's obstetrician, Dr. Angelos Alexander, was in the clinic at that moment. He appeared in just a few minutes, and after a cordial greeting, shocked us by saying that he wanted to admit Angie to the hospital immediately. And furthermore, he was calling in a high-risk specialist as soon as Angie was registered. I went numb all over!

He went on to explain that he believed that Angie was suffering from pre-eclampsia, a disorder where a mother's body rejects her pregnancy as a foreign and highly toxic invasion. Angie's specific condition was a textbook example—high blood pressure, kidney malfunction causing protein in the urine, and swollen ankles and feet. In addition, Angie's placenta was not working at full efficiency, so the baby was not getting sufficient nutrients. The doctor wanted a high-risk pregnancy colleague to develop an immediate plan of action. His final remark was "This baby is going to be delivered much sooner than anticipated." I thought that was a huge understatement since I hadn't planned on a delivery for another two months!

I managed to ask a few questions that I hoped would lead the doctor to a more reasonable and relaxed tone. It backfired.

"Could we go home to get some things for the hospital?"

"No."

"Will Angie be here overnight?

"Angie will not be going home until the baby is born."

Really to myself, but out loud I said, "Who will take care of our twin boys?"

He responded with "Are your mothers available for help?"

Dr. Alexander was gentle and professional, but also authoritative and firm. He gave no assurance that everything was all right, because it obviously wasn't. But he did assure us, repeatedly, that these procedures were the right thing to do. Finally, he said he was confident that if they had to induce labor, the baby would survive. That was what we needed to hear! It was about 3:00 PM. This was the first somewhat hopeful statement we had heard since 9:00 AM that morning. The roller coaster ride was just beginning the massive first descent.

St. Alexius Medical Center is less that a half-mile away from the North Suburban Clinic. The ride over gave us no chance for mental or emotional process. We checked in through the emergency outpatient area, and after fifteen minutes, and what seemed like a hundred forms to sign, were told to report to the maternity ward on the second floor.

I was surprised by the specific content of the forms. Not only did we have to repeat all the information we had already given the doctors on a dozen previous occasions, but we had to release the hospital and its insurance company from absolutely all liability or guarantee of ethical and professional service. Somehow that is what I thought I was counting on not releasing them from! But nevertheless, we signed them.

The silent ride on the elevator to the maternity ward was filled with fear and confusion. Between several brief, silent prayers I tried my best to comfort my wife who was understandably frightened and ignore my own fears and heart rate that had to be beating 150 beats per minute or higher!

We were welcomed warmly by the nurses manning the maternity ward. They took us to a birthing room in the back wing of the ward and said that we would see Dr. Rick Taylor, the high-risk specialist, as soon as he was available around 5:00 PM. It was only 3:30 PM. The room was nicely furnished, but a little small. Later we learned that it was an overflow room.

We called Angie's mother and my mother to inform them of the situation and to ask for their prayers. Then we called Vicki to see if she would be able to take care of the boys for the next several days. She had already forfeited this entire day and assured us she could and would finish the week if necessary! Talk about blessings again!

After that conversation, and after having her maternal instincts satisfied with appropriate care arranged for her two sons, some of

Angie's normal demeanor returned, and in a soft but confident voice she said that although she really wanted a vaginal birth she was ready to deliver via C-section whenever the baby had to come.

Soon, Dr. Taylor's assistant, Stephanie, came to escort us to the high-risk room, and she did so with great tenderness and care. She thoroughly explained what would happen with Dr. Taylor as she helped Angie get ready for the procedure. As Dr. Taylor entered the make-shift ultrasound room, he began a running explanation of what he was doing. His manner was business-like but friendly, low-keyed but serious. And most enlightening and comforting, he told us every few minutes what was happening to Angie and the baby.

First he checked the amniotic fluid level. It was a little on the low end of scale, but not dangerous at the moment. Second he checked the placenta. The position was fine, but he was concerned about the blood flow, which was a sporadic pulsating style of flow, sending a strong stream and then slowly lessening for a couple of beats before repeating the pattern. He watched this for at least ten minutes, reading several screens all the time.

Next he walked us through the baby's entire anatomy and gave us the wonderful news that she looked very strong. She was quite stable, too, despite the instability of the placenta. I have no doubt that he would have been just as direct and forward if the news had been bad. He even took the time to show us that this baby was constantly sucking its thumb!

Angie and I peppered him with questions, and he answered every single question, and even repeated answers with additional information if more clarity was needed. At all times he was calm and gentle, a specialist in his field and a specialist in doctor-patient communications. We were in good hands.

It was nearly an hour before he completed his work, an hour that gave us a much-needed boost in confidence and a sense of preparedness for what might be coming. His closing remarks were straightforward as could be. He was going to recommend that the baby be taken immediately by Cesarean section. The baby was doing fine, but the placenta was not. He was not sure the placenta could sustain any more trauma, and Angie's blood pressure was still way up around 180/95. If they waited at all, it would be only to give Angie a shot of steroids for the baby's lungs and some magnesium sulfate for Angie, to prevent a seizure. The baby's lungs were the only organs that might not be mature enough to handle such a severely premature birth.

He then left the room to find Angie's pediatrician, Dr. Alexander. The ten-minute wait for his return was our first opportunity to gather ourselves and process some of the surprising events of this fitful day. Just nine hours earlier, we had entered the North Suburban Clinic for a routine check-up. And now, with Angie only thirty-three weeks pregnant with a child weighing under four pounds, we were being told they might deliver the baby that night. We prayed together and felt blessed by Dr. Taylor's bedside manner and Stephanie's sweet spirit.

Just a few minutes later, Dr. Taylor reappeared and admitted in so many words that he and Dr. Alexander disagreed on the timetable for delivery. Again, I was impressed with his professional integrity. I was pleased to hear openly what they both were thinking rather than to see any tension, strain, and conflicting non-verbal behavior that might put any more fear in our already scared hearts.

It was, essentially, a matter of professional judgment. Dr. Alexander wanted first to get Angie's blood pressure under control with a magnesium drip, and second to give her a steroid shot for the baby's lungs. Dr. Taylor wanted to deliver the baby immediately because it was the only way to get Angie's blood pressure down and thus prevent a possible terrible seizure that might kill both mother and child. Apparently Dr. Alexander had the final authority because Angie was escorted rapidly to one of the adjacent birthing suites and promptly hooked up to a magnesium sulfate drip.

About an hour later, after we had settled back in our tiny overflow room, Angie was connected to two monitors, one to indicate the baby's heartbeat at all times and the other to measure Angie's own blood pressure. This second device had a cuff around her upper arm to show her blood pressure four times per hour. It was awkward and painful, and Angie couldn't get any rest because the cuff would squeeze the color out of her arm every fifteen minutes. It was about 8:00 PM and looked to be a long night.

While the doctors were getting ready for their next move, Angie and I tried to do the same. Our little planning conference was interrupted, however, when Vicki and Kevin arrived with Eliah and Jacob, who at this point had just turned nine months old. It was exactly what we all needed to lift our spirits.

Angie snuggled with the boys, one at a time, and as if they sensed her fragile condition, they were less wiggly and rambunctious than normal. Then I took the boys for a "proud papa" tour of the hospital. It was precisely the emotional release that I needed. And now, of course, everyone in the building stopped for a minute to say something nice about the adorable identical twins in the extra-long stroller and to inquire whether I was really there for another delivery! They stayed for about an hour.

Finally, about 10:00 PM, we decided it would be best if I went home for the evening. Angie and Dr. Alexander were both confident that despite minimal reduction in her blood pressure readings she was not in any grave danger for the evening. It was certainly still a very high-risk pregnancy, but the immediate crisis had been brought under control. Several of the nurses suggested, too, that I go home. They reminded me that this was probably the only night in the foreseeable future that delivery was not likely to happen.

After a prayer together and one of those third- or fourth-date twenty-minute goodbyes, I left the building, found my car in the sea of concrete and steel, and drove off into the night. As is often the case with me, the tears came freely once I was alone in complete silence with no husband, father, friend or counselor role to play.

When I arrived home, I quietly prepared the morning shift for the boys. Bottles had to be made, finger food laid out, high chairs prepped, and bibs put in place. (To avoid hurt feelings each morning, I had to carry both boys at the same time from their bedroom to the kitchen.)

Finally I got into bed myself for the evening, and it hit me that this was the culminating moment of the unbelievable year of mental and emotional exhaustion. After a long period of processing and analyzing, I prayed myself to sleep within minutes. Two energetic baby boys would be yelling for me in six hours, and I knew that this was probably my best chance for uninterrupted and restful sleep for the rest of the week, if not the rest of the year!

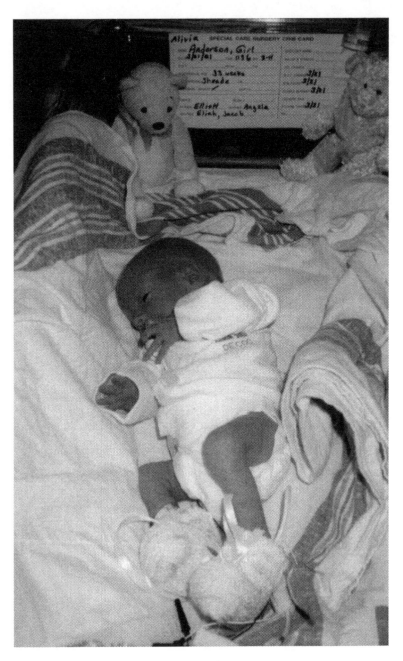

ALIVIA IN SPECIAL CARE CRIB—5 DAYS OLD, ST. ALEXIUS

CHAPTER 17

Too Soon,
But Just in Time

The next morning, the 20th of March, I got the boys settled in their chairs with their bottles and some Cheerios™, and then called the hospital to get a report on Angie. It had not been a good night for her. Her blood pressure had at two different times climbed to dangerous levels, but came down again a while later. The hospital staff chose not to change her schedule.

This news altered my plan to attend our regular Tuesday morning President's Cabinet meeting. I took Jacob with me to inform the President, update my colleagues, and to receive a prayer. Then I went to my office to talk with Terri about the work for the rest of the week. We both knew I would not be back soon. All total, we were on campus for about an hour. Then I dropped Jacob off back at home with Vicki and went to the hospital with a couple days' worth of clothing and personal necessities for Angie and me.

Angie was glad to see me and admitted that the night had

been very difficult. An hour or so after I arrived, Angie was moved to a normal birthing suite. It was a pleasant environment with the birthing cubicle placed prominently in the natural visual path of the expecting mother's bed. I knew that Angie was in the closing stretch. Even the recliner in this suite was comfortable, and there was a lot of space on each side of the bed for additional nursing staff at the time of delivery. The only problem was the noise level of the construction work going on all over the entire hospital.

As the day progressed Angie's blood pressure went down enough for the doctor's assistants to prepare her for inducement. Dr. Alexander came by several times and she also was seen by Dr. Taylor twice. They were in the midst of one of those delivery streaks that all the nurses swear is based on the position of the moon, the barometric pressure, approaching warm fronts, or some other change in the weather.

Around lunchtime, Dr. Alexander told us he would deliver the baby that evening. He explained that although Angie was doing better, there really was no reason to put off the inevitable. An early delivery was the only road to recovery for Angie and the only sure way to save the baby. We were all for those two realities, so we eagerly agreed to be ready on a moment's notice.

We spent the next few hours in mental adjustments and phone calls to our families. Then around 4:30 PM Dr. Alexander popped into the room to tell us he had changed his mind. He said that he was going to wait until the next morning (Wednesday) to start

Angie on Pitocin in preparation for an induced delivery. His ratio-nale was that he wanted to give the baby another day and to give Angie an evening's rest.

Angie and I both offered some mild resistance to that plan, explaining that we had already switched gears and were ready for tonight. It was just a hunch, but I think the delay was as much for Dr. Alexander as it was for us. He was running on empty, having delivered eight babies in the past two days. A seasoned veteran, he surely knew his own limits, and if he needed a night's rest, I was with him all the way.

Angie was clearly losing her strength, however. Besides going on two days of nothing to eat but ice chips, the previous week had been strenuous, with the boys suffering from a flu bug and not sleeping like they normally did. With her sleep interrupted every hour, she was mentally and physical exhausted, and not at all ready for the trauma of a premature birthing process.

She couldn't get much sleep at the hospital either, and for the next two hours she dozed in and out of restless sleep. Around 9:00 PM, she got a real emotional lift when Brock and their mother arrived. They provided the powerful emotional bond that exists at a higher level in blood relatives.

Without either of them saying a word, there was a conscious exchange of grace and acceptance. I heard it evolve in the soft tones of their voices, and I saw it take shape in their hugs and in their eyes. At a time when Angie was broken and discouraged, her mom held and caressed her and assured her that she could do it and would do it, and that she would take care of her and stay with us until she was at full strength again.

I felt almost embarrassed to be in the room. I motioned to Brock and we left the room to get some snacks and allow the two women this private moment. I knew Susie was frightened and probably cried all the way back to our house, but for those twenty minutes she was the queen mother and wore her royalty with honor.

Angie was visibly stronger after her mom and brother left, so we figured that while she was in a positive mood we should narrow down the list of names we had been working on for the past several months. We had originally agreed upon Abigail, but the Gums had just named their new baby Abigail, so we removed that one from our list.

I always liked Areal and had a found a river in the Old Testament times called Aria that I liked, and Angie wanted Kia, but since we couldn't tolerate each other's selections we were at ground zero. We wanted the name to begin with an "A," and I had a desire for a name with three syllables. Then I could introduce our children as Eliah, Jacob and "la-la-la." I thought it sounded better and had more natural rhythm. I'm sure I'm not the only parent to struggle with a final name choice for such an insignificant and random reason.

Eventually we settled on three options and decided to wait to see our new little girl face to face to identify her personality. I'd heard several mothers say they changed the name the minute they laid eyes on their new baby, so we thought we'd be safe with three options when the time came.

The name selection dialogue took nearly two hours, and it really helped pass the time. Angie was now having occasional contractions that got fairly intense, so from time to time we stopped talking. Angie would then breathe through the pain while I dabbed her forehead with a cool washcloth. We drifted off to sleep around midnight. My easy chair was no longer as comfortable, but it was still a decent host, and Angie let me sleep for a couple of one- or two-hour periods, even with her sporadic painful contractions.

I woke up a little after 4:00 AM because I was hungry. Angie was sleeping peacefully, and the lights from the parking lot below bathed her face in a soft, angelic glow. I didn't make a move. She needed the rest, and I was determined not to make any noise, no matter how hungry I was. I didn't even shift my weight in the recliner.

About twenty minutes passed before Nurse Bernice came in to check on her. She had to awaken Angie to read the monitors, look for swollen joints, and take another blood pressure test. They had removed the cuff the night before, so at least Angie didn't have to go through that nuisance so often. They were still taking blood pressure readings every three to five hours, but that seemed like half a day compared to the cuff system. I was thankful for the opportunity to run get a snack from the visitors' room.

At 7:00 AM Angie got the injection of Pitocin that Dr. Alexander had ordered, and Bernice told her she should start feeling contractions that would build over the next couple of hours. Bernice seemed to be surprised, but not worried, when Angie told her that she had already felt several mild and several significant contractions throughout the evening.

The cafeteria was now open, so I went down and ate an enormous meal. My fast metabolism is probably tied to my hyperactivity, and the last three days of nervous tension had made me feel hungry all the time. Then too, I eat more when I'm scared or anxious. My blood sugar fluctuates too much, I suppose, because I can't seem to go more than three hours without food. Angie also has a quick metabolism, and she had had no food for nearly thirty hours! I felt sorry for her and tried to eat away from her sight, but I had to follow my normal nutrition habits or we would both have been without any strength. She asked me about my choices, but was not too disappointed because she is not a big breakfast eater anyway. We spent the rest of the morning waiting for the Pitocin to work.

At exactly 11:00 AM Angie made a strange and eerie noise that seemed to be a physiological response to something completely out of her control. It sounded like a cross between an "uh oh" and a gasp, with just the sound of the air and the "oh" vowel echoing through the room. I was pacing around the room when I heard it and whipped my head around to see Angie's startled expression.

"I felt a release," she exclaimed tentatively.

"All right. I'll take a look." Bernice responded, as she came over instantly.

"Maybe your water broke, although it would be a bit early," she offered.

Bernice lifted the sheet and everyone except Angie saw a big pool of dark red blood. I almost vomited and my knees buckled, as I felt a wave of nausea and a rush of fear sweep over my body. Angie saw my reaction and this time anxiously asked Bernice what the trouble was. Calm as could be, Bernice cleaned up Angie as she explained that a discharge of blood often occurs before the baby starts south. I was so glad Bernice was there. If I had been the one to discover the blood I probably would have screamed and ran hysterically out of the room and headed towards the cafeteria for yet another meal!

No sooner had she covered Angie back up and returned to business, when Angie spoke up again.

"I just felt another release."

This second flow was heavier than the first, and it was even darker, a maroon shade. Puzzled this time, Bernice called for another nurse as she went through the cleaning routine again. I had a painful, twisted knot in my stomach by this time. I had no idea what was happening, but it sure looked like Angie and the baby were both in serious trouble.

Bernice sent out an immediate call for Dr. Alexander. Then, as they cleaned up Angie again, and wondered aloud what all this meant, Angie had a third release, by far the heaviest and most fearsome. The nurses were visibly shaken this time, and very concerned that Dr. Alexander had not yet acknowledged getting the call.

By this time I was in a state of total panic and trying desperately not to let Angie notice. I couldn't hold back any longer, so I rushed out into the hallways in search of Dr. Alexander myself. When I reached the main corridor, I stopped at the snack room to grab an apple. I opened the door right into the back of a man who was on his cell phone. I apologized and took a step toward the refrigerator when I realized it was Dr. Alexander. I blurted out as politely as I could, but with conviction and volume, that my wife needed him right away because she was bleeding. As I turned to leave the room, I grabbed a handful of crackers that were in a basket by the door. God even uses our addictive coping mechanisms for His timing and purposes!

I hurried back to Angie's room and told the nurses that Dr. Alexander was on his way. He came through the door right after me, grabbed a chair, and wheeled himself to the foot of the bed. He received a latex glove from one of the three nurses now at his side, and told Angie he had to determine the condition of her uterus. His demeanor was firm, quiet, and confident, the kind of manner we all want from our doctor in a time of crisis.

He probed for twenty seconds, took off the latex glove, looked Angie right in the eye, and said, "Your placenta has abrupted." He then explained that "abruption" means the placenta has torn loose from the uterine wall and he would have to do an emergency Cesarean right away. It seemed perfectly clear to me that both mother and child were in serious danger.

He stood up, gave the nurses several directives, and left the room to find another doctor, a specialist who would be a part of this critical operation. Bernice and the other nurses started flying around the room, disconnecting wires, prepping Angie's abdomen, and unplugging machines. They had obviously been through all this kind of thing before, but their urgency was not helping either of our spirits.

In the middle of all the activity, the phone rang. I picked it up and it was Terri. She asked for an update. I told her in ten seconds what was going on, and asked her to please have the Judson staff pray for Angie and the baby and me. I feel certain that the timing of the call was not just a coincidence. God was with us, and the prayers that arose from throughout the Judson campus and our church body were definitely felt the rest of the day.

I followed the gurney down the hallway and into the operation area. When we entered the operating room, a nurse told me I would have to leave. Dr. Alexander protested, but the nurse held firm and I was escorted out of the area. I didn't get a chance to hug Angie, to kiss her, or to tell her that I loved her. The nurse then told me to scrub up and put on a full gown. She would send for me when I could join Angie for support. Just like that we were separated, isolated, and alone.

Would Angie survive? Was the baby still alive? What if all went well, and then the baby died in two weeks? What if I lost them both? Who would help me raise Eliah and Jacob? How could the nurse leave me alone at this terrifying moment? How could I not be at Angie's side during this terrifying operation?

In a few minutes that seemed like an hour, I went to a vacant room and called Susie. After a brief update, I asked her to call my mother. There was no way I could have talked to my mother right then without bursting into tears, and I didn't want to rejoin Angie without getting myself composed. I went back to my spot in the hallway. I stared across the hall at the wall numbly and prayed— with my eyes wide open—for the doctors, for Angie, for the baby, and for my ability to handle appropriately whatever was about to occur. I tried to avoid thinking about life without Angie.

Just then Nurse Weber came around the corner of the hallway. We had been calling each other every few hours for updates, so I had asked her to come to be with Angie after the Pitocin had started to take effect that morning. Susan, of course, knew what abruption was, and explained to me what the doctors were likely doing at that moment. Just then, the drill sergeant nurse, who had kicked me out of the area earlier, called me back into the operating room with not a much different tone. I obeyed and followed.

It's a good thing I have a weak gag reflex because as soon as I entered the room Dr. Alexander sliced Angie's belly with a scalpel. I staggered and stopped cold. A kinder and gentler nurse rushed over and gently led me to a stool behind the large sheet that separated Angie's torso and head from the vulgarity and brutality of the operation. Angie's arms were spread wide, straight out from the shoulders, and strapped down at the wrists to prevent her from instinctively reaching for her stomach during the assault on her body.

I was stunned. Frozen in fear. I just sat there, looking at Angie's face and rubbing her forehead softly. I was trying to remember to breathe and to concentrate on everything except my anxiety.

This was difficult because the sounds of a Caesarean section are ghostly, with a juicy gurgling of fluids and blood as the organs are untangled to free up the uterus. Then in what seemed like a resounding thud, Angie's uterus was catapulted up and on to her rib cage.

The secondary sounds are just as memorable: the clicking and slicing of the cutting utensils, the low, muffled conversation of the two doctors (with, from the assisting physician, a few surprising Chicago street-level profanities), and the squeaks and shuffles of gym shoes and gowns as the staff hustled back and forth, around and about. It was a gruesome soundtrack that I still hear when my thoughts flash back to that day. It's amazing what your senses rely on for memory processing when your visual field is blocked or eliminated.

Then, just when I had almost forgotten what the entire morning was all about, out of the corner of my eye I saw a small, bloody ball of flesh carried quickly, but carefully, to the warming area. Was that our baby? Was she alive? Was she all there, ears and nose, fingers and toes? Was Angie OK?

Suddenly, there was a hand on my shoulder and I nearly jumped through the ceiling. I turned to see Angela, our Jamaican nurse, the first nurse we had on our check-in day, announce that we had a healthy baby girl. And, as if on cue, our new little girl made a few startled noises. Her lungs were not very strong yet, so all she could manage was a soft muffled shriek and a few tiny groans. But it was sweet music to our ears.

She was just a naked, curled-up package of purple wrinkled skin, seemingly no bigger than a newborn puppy, but a work of art to me. The nurses were cleaning her up and handling her rather aggressively, I thought, as they put her through a battery of tests. They were getting to handle and manipulate our new baby before Angie and I had even really looked at her. I felt a little left out.

One of the nurses said from behind the veil that they were putting mother Angie back together again. Her bleeding had stopped. I heaved a sigh of relief. I had heard that hemorrhaging is one of the main difficulties in Cesarean sections, and since Angie had lost a lot of blood before the operation, her doctors were super alert to that issue once the baby was cleared.

As they stapled Angie's stomach back together, I risked a small piece of communication with her, and told her that the baby was beautiful. Angie was very alert now, "Can I see my new baby?" she asked to anyone who was listening.

One of the nurses was close enough to overhear the request. "Of course you can." Angie was still strapped in, so the nurse placed the baby near Angie's face for a few sighs and kisses.

Then the nurse turned to me and said, "Do you want to carry your daughter to the neonatal care area?" She obviously had no knowledge of my track record for stumbling and bumbling in non-athletic arenas, and somehow she trusted that I could handle the job. I looked at Angie. She gave me a nod of approval (without which I would have declined), and I rushed over to the nurse's side to accept the child.

An enormous weight of fear and anxiety left my body as the tiny bundle was put in my arms. She weighed only 3 lbs. 11 oz., and her face was but a shadow to her big, round, blue eyes. After carrying the bulky, squirmy boys around the house for the past several months, this little being seemed so light and fragile that I was afraid she would break if I held her too tightly.

That first, delicate walk with my new daughter was supervised by Dotty, the attending neonatal nurse, who was in charge those first few hours. I gladly handed my daughter over to her when we were inside the protected baby area. I wondered if I had done any damage during the 100-foot trek. When they unwrapped her to put in the monitors and feeding tubes, I was amazed at how tiny she was. She was so skinny, yet so tough. She didn't seem to mind the probing and prodding as the nurses finished up their initial readings. I was just so thankful that she was alive. I was overwhelmed with emotion, but a day or two away from its expression. It was at that moment I knew what I thought her name should be.

I hurried back to the operating room to find Angie still on the table, but free of her shackles, and now much calmer. There was an exhausted look of relief on her face, and she continuously licked her lips and asked me to get her some water. I told her that I thought we should name her Alivia with an A. She liked the name and said she would confirm it when she saw her girl in person.

NORMAL FEEDING TIME ACTIVITY, 2001

CHAPTER 18

Three to Get Ready

Alivia's first ninety minutes out of the womb were spent in an oxygen tent. Her color and responses indicated that she was as normal and healthy as a thirty-three-week preemie could be. In the meantime, Angie had been moved to another care room for morphine to block out the pain roaring through her damaged body.

When I came back from my second trip to admire Alivia, I ran into Judson's president and provost, Jerry Cain and Dale Simmons. They were not aware that Angie had just been through an emergency C-section. I gave them the whole story as accurately as any stressed-out, totally exhausted, big-picture, nervous dad could. They had actually already seen Angie when they had been in the hallway looking for us. Her gurney was wheeled by as she came out of the operating room. Evidently, the front desk nurses didn't all realize that Angie had gone to surgery because I can't imagine they would have sent two non-family visitors back to see a mother who had just finished an emergency C-section. Maybe the doctor titles fooled them.

Anyway, I felt a wonderful sense of security realizing that Angie went into surgery with a Judson friend as our last contact, and she came out of surgery with Judson friends waiting. The interconnectedness of the Christian culture and the unity in the spirit of believers transcends time and space. It sounds a little weighty and overstated, but it is true.

Angie was desperate to see and hold Alivia again, but the nurses insisted that she rest and gain strength first. This left dad in charge of the early bonding, and I welcomed the opportunity to spread my wings as a caretaker. My first task was to learn how to change her diaper. I was glad for the experience with Eliah and Jacob, but this was a little more involved. Alivia required pre-change weigh-ins and post-change weigh-ins. Preemies lose weight right after birth, and if they don't start to gain weight in a day or two, something might be wrong. So the doctor in charge reads the weight charts often.

My second task was to take a lot of pictures and videotapes. It was a joy to do. I had already filmed ten video hours of the boys in their first nine months of life, so carrying the camera was becoming second nature. I took many shots of Alivia alone, but looked forward to the first picture with mother and daughter.

Her official time of delivery was 11:21 AM. This means that just twenty-one minutes after Angie announced that she had released something, Alivia was born. A couple of hours after the crisis, Dr. Alexander explained to us that the placenta had almost completely separated from Angie's uterine wall. If it had been a one hundred percent abruption, there might have been no chance at all for a successful delivery. As it was, he estimated that Alivia had only three or four minutes left in the sac without brain damage at the time of her delivery.

Moreover, if we hadn't appeared for the seven-month checkup two days early, and if Angie had been home alone when the abruption occurred, both Angie and the baby might have died in a very short time. It just seemed so obvious that God had had his hand on us and has granted us His tender mercies throughout this whole wild parenting journey.

Grandma Susie was the first family visitor to see Alivia. Next came my sister, Karin, and our friend, Steve Baumann, both of whom could not hold Alivia, but were able to ooh and ahh appropriately from the viewing window. Karin and Steve also delivered Angie's request for a milk shake from Steak and Shake. The request was a little unusual for Angie, who didn't really care much for ice cream and even more so since she had gone two days without food. After two small swallows, she threw it all up, and decided to follow the doctor's orders on a properly prescribed diet. I enjoyed the abandoned treat instead!

The morphine had Angie euphoric, but her swelling was still severe and her color was poor. Also, the doctors were still concerned about her blood pressure. It was not coming down as quickly as they thought it would, so they restricted her movement, physical exertion, and even the number of visitors she could see.

That night, despite frequent checks and blood pressure readings, Angie slept well and long. I was back in one of the uncomfortable chairs, but I slept like a baby. It's amazing how much our sleep is affected by our moods, and more specifically, our stress. Now that Angie and Alivia were out of immediate danger, I could have slept through an earthquake, a hospital bombing, or severe calf cramps, and probably even hunger pangs. I was now the father of three beautiful children after wondering for nearly ten years if I would ever be a father at all.

Around 10:00 AM the next morning, the 22nd of March, they moved Angie to an overflow maternity area, confirming our suspicion about how busy this maternity ward really was. It turned out well, though, because she was now closer to the nursery. She settled down in this new room, and promptly threw up again. Within a few hours she was feeling much better. Finally, at 2:00 PM she was ready to see her daughter in full glory for the first time.

I wheeled Angie into the nursery and up to Alivia's cubicle. I assisted the nurse in the weigh-in procedures and then handed Alivia to Angie. After seven months together, then three days of chaotic birthing procedures, mother and daughter were together, safe and secure. This started a pattern of one-hour visits every three hours. That is all they would allow both mother and daughter as they recovered. The mother-child bond began to establish itself outside the womb.

Despite the joy of spending time with her baby, Angie was still nauseous. She begged them for serious food until the nurse consented and brought her some legitimate items for supper. Her queasy stomach might have been partly related to her body rejecting the high levels of medication as it asked for solid food and substantial liquids. She ate a few Saltine™ crackers and felt the best she had in a week. When the crackers stayed down, Angie fielded a couple of phone calls, and then took a nap.

When she awoke, we tried to watch television and just relax as a constant stream of visitors came by to see Alivia. I gladly accepted my role of the tour guide and the proud displayer of the new princess as they could only look through the window. I enjoyed telling and re-telling the story, even in abbreviated form, to one and all.

Around 8 PM our peace and tranquility were jeopardized yet once again. When would we get a 24-hour period without a crisis? Grandma Susie called to give us an update on Eliah and Jacob and to tell us that she now had the flu, no doubt a mixture of stress and leftover germs from the boys, who had the virus the week before. She needed me to come home immediately. I packed up my things, kissed Angie good night and took off for Elgin. During the drive home, the reality of the past four days sank in, and I had an overwhelming sense of gratitude and relief. I sang and cried and prayed and rejoiced in what the Lord had done for my family.

The next morning, however, came all too soon. While the boys and I had pancakes, I called Angie at the hospital. The doctors were still monitoring her blood pressure, which had not yet returned to normal. Otherwise her incision was healing nicely and her general recovery was on schedule. She was eager to attempt to breastfeed Alivia in the early afternoon.

I wasn't even close to being ready to return to work at the college, but still felt the need to check a few of my messages. There were no emergencies, and my staff seemed to have all normal operations under control. I was glad for a break from at least one area of our existence and thankful for a great group of friends I worked with.

Susie slept that morning until about 9 AM, an eternity for her, which meant she had slept about fifteen straight hours. She was still not able to do a whole lot, but felt well enough to drink some orange juice and greet the boys. She then quickly returned to the upstairs bedroom to finish recuperating.

Late that afternoon, my sister, Karin, stopped by the house. We loaded up the boys in the van and headed down to the hospital to see my two other angels. When we arrived, we took the boys to the maternity ward, then to the visitors' room in the nursery area. We let them play and roll around while Angie and I took turns holding Alivia in the adjacent room. The nurse said that

Alivia's sucking reflex was the best she had seen from a preemie in eighteen years of working at the hospital! That thumb-sucking womb skill was preparation for her early arrival!

So a short time later, Alivia took to the breast very easily, and it was just a matter of time before she and Angie fell into a comfortable breastfeeding rhythm. In fact, Alivia's development surprised everyone on the ward. She suffered none of the problems so common to preemie babies in their first few days out of the womb. It was a blessing, and allowed Angie to get back on her feet more quickly.

On Saturday, the 24th of March, Dr. Alexander told Angie she was stable enough to go home. Angie was not emotionally ready, however. After several tearful conversations with the nurses, she received Dr. Alexander's permission to stay for one more day. Susie was back at full strength, and we assured Angie that we would be fine at home without her. She needed a little more rest before tackling her new family of three babies less than one year of age!

On Sunday, the 25th of March, late in the morning, reluctantly she agreed to come home. Susie and I, joined by Grandpa Bob and the boys, went down to the hospital to pack Angies things and all of the flower arrangements. There was one problem, though; Alivia did not get to come with us. It was not easy for Angie. She cried off and on all the way home. The boys made up for some of the sadness when they bombarded her with squeals and shrieks, and babbled to her all the way back to Elgin in the van.

At home the boys continued their welcome-back activities, crawling all around to bring her toys and books. On orders from Dr. Alexander, Angie could not lift the boys for any reason for six weeks while her incision was healing. So, after Susie assured Angie she'd stay in Elgin as long as necessary, we settled into an efficient routine of duties. In addition, in yet another generous gesture of friendship, Vicki and Kevin canceled their vacation plans to help us through this transition period.

The remainder of the week was filled with as many trips to the hospital as we could manage. I went back to work at the college on Tuesday and would run down to the hospital every night with Angie so she could nurse and bond with Alivia. This evening trip was Angie's second trip each day. She was with Alivia for a four-hour block that covered two rounds of care each day, neighbors and friends took her for the 10 AM to 2 PM trip, and I took her for the 5 PM to 9 PM trip. Wow! Friends and family sure are important during these significant life events.

Finally, and in order to bring Alivia home, we had to follow all the standard operating procedures for premature babies. First, she had to gain weight; although there is no longer a specific mandated weight in our county and state, four pounds is a minimum they still follow. Second, because her bilirubins were fluctuating, she had to spend some time beneath the warming lights. Third, she had to show consistent bowel functions and feeding patterns. Fourth, she had to pass the state-required sleep apnea test.

At the end of a couple of stressful weeks, with her parents running back and forth, to and from the hospital, Alivia passed all the tests and was able to come home. The day was April 3, 2001: one year **exactly** from the day Becky called to tell us we had been selected by the birthparents and were going to be adoptive parents to twin boys.

Can you believe that? After ten years of waiting, we now had three babies in our care and had received all of them within one year. And they were separated in age by only nine months and four days! God works in mysterious ways, and those mysterious ways were clearly evident in our crowded home.

OUR FAMILY, BOYS FIRST BIRTHDAY, ALIVIA 3 MONTHS

Chapter 19

Tougher Than Triplets

We placed a bassinet for Alivia in the corner of our bedroom. The boys followed their schedule like obedient little soldiers, and we did not want to risk any interruption in their routine. Alivia was on a three-hour feeding timetable complete with much crying and fussing. Since Angie was nursing her, the proximity to the bassinet was convenient and necessary. For the first month home, Angie had to take care of the early-morning shifts for all three babies so that I could get enough sleep to effectively finish up the end-of-the-school year procedures.

We slowly implemented nap times for Alivia in the third crib in the baby room, but the boys were keenly aware of a stranger in their midst. It's amazing how much noise one of the boys could make without disturbing his twin brother in the least. Bring in a different sound, however, like Alivia's occasional timid whimpering, and both boys would wake up immediately. This was a further recognition of "twin bonding," which we learned quickly is an ever-present component in twin growth and development.

Grandma Susie stayed with us another five days and helped us adjust to the new schedule and patterns of responsibility. Dr. Alexander had cautioned Angie against trying to lift the boys, for any reason whatsoever, so Vicki, Susie, and I handled the boys exclusively. Angie would sit on the carpet floor or lie on the couch, and we would place the boys in her lap so she could still snuggle and bond with then. They were obviously displeased that Angie would not pick them up, so whenever she sat down they would crawl all over her with a vengeance.

It was a wonderful, but highly emotional weekend when Angie's father arrived back in Elgin again, this time to take Susie back to Iowa. The goodbye was difficult. I assured them that I could and would take care of the three babies while Angie recovered her full strength, but both mothers felt apprehensive about the separation. During that whole month of stress and strain, Susie's commitment to her daughter and our family was crucial. It was Mom and Grandma to the rescue, and we were blessed to have her available and willing!

Alivia's coming home to our three-ring circus immediately threw us back into a constant state of sleep deprivation. Taking care of one baby is a fulltime job, and with our unique scenario it led to a grueling summer. The tight schedule we had for two was now impossible for all three. The variables and timings involved threw off the whole system. When friends observed, "It's like having triplets, isn't it?" our response was usually, "No, not really. Triplets would be on the same time intervals. Alivia and the boys are on almost opposite feed-play-sleep schedules, so there is never a down period." It went on that way well into Alivia's six month.

Our around-the-clock daily schedule demanded that we learn how to sleep a few hours at a time. Angie nursed Alivia every three hours those first few weeks, but because of her preemie size and inability to hold all of her milk down followed by Angie's necessary pumping, the interval was really only one and a half hours apart. After the 11:00 PM feeding was over around 12:30 AM, Angie could sleep until almost 2:00 AM and then sleep again from 3:30 AM until the 5:00 AM feeding. In addition, Angie had to always hold Alivia upright for about an hour after eating due to her digestive issues, so many of those sleeping periods were done sitting up!

Eliah and Jacob started their day about 5:30 AM. I'd get up to take care of their entire early morning needs—breakfast, two diaper changes each, morning dressing, an hour of free play, twenty minutes of reading books, and, if needed, one video. Then I'd put them down for their morning nap around 8:00 AM.

After Alivia's 6:30 AM nursing session, which included a diaper change and some play time, Angie would try to pick up another couple hours of sleep. At 8:30 AM I would leave for work. By this time, Vicki would have turned on her monitor upstairs to be ready for whoever needed her first. On days when Vicki was working for her other family, we would have a variety of volunteers help out.

As she did when we first brought the boys home, Terri organized a meal calendar with the Judson community to provide us with four evening meals per week. When I'd get home from work at 5 PM, all three babies were expecting to be fed at the same time. This meant that Angie and I had to feed, bathe, and put them to bed before we could get to our own meal. The nights it was left to our own cooking, it was often 8:00 PM before we ate. The meals from our community helped us eat a little as we worked. After the boys were in their cribs, we would take turns taking care of Alivia while doing household chores like the laundry, dishes, bills, phone calls, and getting prepared for the next day's duties.

Overall, a typical day consisted of twenty-two diaper changes, fourteen bottles for the boys, six nursing sessions for Alivia followed by six pumpings, five changes of clothes, four short walks with the babies in strollers, two loads of laundry, and one brief family outing to a local park playground, the Judson fitness center, or the mall—sometimes ending with a sanity ride in the van around Elgin!

Finally, we reached a milestone, when in early September, Alivia began to sleep through the night and naturally align herself with her brothers' schedule. She loved to watch her brothers and would almost jump out of my arms to follow their play activities. Every moment of every day she wanted to know where they were and what they were doing. She had adjusted her own biorhythms to match theirs, and she would cut her own naptime short to be a part of the action. It seemed to be a specific, conscious effort on her part. I think she thought they were indeed triplets!

I can't describe the strange mixture of overwhelming joy in finally having children and the equally overwhelming dread of being trapped in an endless, tedious routine. The fatigue alone can erode your positive energy and leave you on the other end of the spectrum from the infertility pain. I hate to admit it, but several times I reminisced about life without them. It was a guilt-ridden mental moment or two, but it was real. We were totally wiped out physically, emotionally, mentally, and spiritually.

The schedule, however, does become a source of comfort and security at the same time. But because of that, anything that throws you off schedule becomes an archenemy. And any few moments you could seize for yourself become exquisite relief. Mowing the yard, for example, turned into my own private emotional refuge. In just one slow year, we went from being an active married couple, productive and involved in the community, to being a couple who were fortunate to make it to church on Sunday. Even when we did attend, we'd often collapse in exhaustion in the chairs at the back of the sanctuary and doze in and out until the closing hymn.

Angie and I were handling all those new responsibilities with the unconditional love and sacrificial parent mentality we had both prayed for. Because of that concession, however, moments of respite could be moments of stress as we negotiated for time to work on our own little personal projects that were always on hold. This book was one such project during the first two years. I ran selfishly to the book whenever all of the children were down for the night.

I can now understand how small children sometimes create intimacy cracks in a marriage. Angie and I worked intentionally and deliberately to ensure that our union was fed and nurtured during this season of baby abundance. The joy and emotional rewards of three children in one year were fantastic, but the wear-and-tear on the marriage was unbelievable.

V. THE ADDITIONAL BLESSING

MATT AND ELIAH; MILLI AND JACOB, FALL 2002

MATT AND ELIAH

CHAPTER 20

Again, LORD?

In early November of 2001, six months after Alivia came home from the hospital, I convinced Angie to go with me to a conference in Palm Springs, California. This was the first time she was apart from all three children at the same time. I knew, despite her denial, that she needed some separation from the babies, and we always had fun traveling together. This was the kind of trip we had planned to take a year earlier before the Alivia surprise was upon us!

It was so strange to be in the plane in a quiet atmosphere, then at the hotel alone, and then to stroll around Palm Springs without a triple stroller, two diaper bags, a bunch of baby snacks, two cameras, and lots of natural stress. It took two days to adjust to the freedom!

The Council of Independent Colleges conference that fall was a joint meeting with Chief Student Affairs Officers and Chief Academic Officers. Thankfully, Dale Simmons, Judson's Provost and Vice President of Academic Affairs, is not a dry academician. He has a wry sense of humor and is fun to be around. Angie and I enjoyed getting to know him outside our academic connection. The entire conference was a valuable professional experience.

Palm Springs also happened to be where one of my good friends and fellow Trinity Evangelical Divinity School alums, Carey Alstadt, lived. We spent a wonderful evening with Carey and his wife, Laura, in their home at the base of a mountain range. And we celebrated together when the Diamondbacks defeated the Yankees in game 7 of the 2001 World Series.

The next afternoon, Monday the 5th of November, we were walking along the streets of Palm Springs when I suddenly noticed that Angie didn't look well. Earlier on the trip she had complained that her fingers felt puffy—and a week prior she had had a couple of nosebleeds. We assumed it was allergies or extreme fatigue on her system. Now, however, she had sections of splotchy skin on the side of her face and down her neck. It must be the sunlight, I thought to myself, but it didn't go away when we were in the shade!

Later that evening, while having dinner on the patio of an upscale Mexican restaurant called Del Rio's, I began to feel a knot in the pit of my stomach. From the moment I had noticed Angie's blemished skin, I had a premonition what the problem was and it made me irritable and suspicious the rest of the day. So there we were having a fine meal in a beautiful restaurant—outside in

November—by ourselves—something we hadn't done in over a year—and I was being a pain in the neck in every way.

Finally, Angie had had enough of my bad attitude and sarcastic remarks. "What is your problem?" she said. "You've been in a bad mood all day and I'm sick of it!"

"You're pregnant again!" I blurted out, thankful that we were out on the patio so my near shouting was carried off with the wind.

Angie absorbed my surprising declaration, folded her napkin, looked off into the sunset, and said calmly, "Impossible." The first surprise pregnancy with Alivia had caught us off guard and we had indeed not been careful during that season because of all of the years without conception. This time around, though, with Alivia still nursing we had felt confident that we were safeguarded. We had no real way of determining her cycle because it had not returned yet, so we tried to come up with some other reason for her condition. We considered every angle, but could not come up with a plausible explanation and ate the rest of the meal shocked and dumbfounded.

By the time we had finished dessert, we were eerily excited. It was a similar feeling to wanting to know what you got on your SATs. You knew you needed to know, and were fairly confident, but weren't really sure you wanted to deal with the consequences of the score. We rushed to pay our bill, hustled over to the corner drug store, purchased a home pregnancy test, and hurried back to our hotel room in a state of nervous exhilaration.

How in the world could this happen to us again? We had been careful and were certainly not planning on another baby now, maybe not ever again biologically, because of the dangerous circumstances of Alivia's birth. Another pregnancy now would mean that we'd have four children less than two years of age by mid-summer of 2002. Agghhhhhhh!!!

Angie tore open the do-it-yourself pregnancy test and followed all the instructions. I badgered her into leaving the bathroom and staying away for a couple of minutes, so we both could see the results at the same time. It was the kind of test that showed a purple line for a positive result—just like the one we had taken a year ago when we found out about Alivia.

It was about 8:15 PM when we decided to read the next line in our ever-growing and complex future. We held hands and tiptoed to the bathroom and anxiously gazed at the apparatus lying on the counter.

ALIVIA, PAIGE, JACOB, ELIAH, AND ALISON RAHN

LIV, PAIGE, ELIAH, JACOB ON INDOOR ROLLERCOASTER 2003

Chapter 21

Four to Go

Angie and I backed away from the sink counter as if we had seen a mouse, a ghost, or an angel of the Lord, not a four-inch strip of paper with a purple line on it.

"I told you, Honey. I knew you were pregnant again," I said between gasps of breath. I felt like I was going to faint, so I back peddled to the bed to sit down.

"It must be a bad reading," Angie said, reaching for the second test we'd purchased at the drug store. I think she had planned to take a second test, for verification, all along. I fell back on the bed, stared at the ceiling and pondered the ramifications of that purple-colored paper. Could we honestly survive another baby right now? Would Angie physically be able to carry one? Could I emotionally handle another life to be responsible for when my own was in spin cycle already?!?

Angie took the test again and then flopped down on the bed next to me with a huge smile on her face. Was she psychotic? Who was this alien creature next to me? She seemed actually excited about this news! Was she a glutton for self-sacrifice and masochistic living? She was already holding such an incredible load of repetitious baby care. How could she imagine another hunk of flesh completely dependent on her and not want to fall to her knees in tears? But instead of any of that kind of emotion and reaction, she was smiling and laughing like we had just won the lottery!

As we waited for the results of the second test—which of course turned out to be positive also—we decided initially not to tell family and friends. We each agreed to inform one special friend, but swear them to secrecy! Angie, in her euphoric condition, needed to tell someone right then, right now! Surprisingly to me, at least, she called a relatively new friend, Beth Kohler. Beth and Angie had become close friends over the last six months or so, and unbeknownst to me had actually laughed at the notion of another pregnancy just weeks before. I wouldn't have found it funny then, and I still wasn't in the mood to laugh now, though God's timing in this babypalooza was certainly ironic and puzzling.

Beth and her husband Tom had four children also, and a year earlier had gone through a situation very similar to our new reality. Beth got pregnant right after they had adopted their first baby, and fourth child overall. That biological child, by coincidence, is named Elliott and was born right after Alivia. I met Beth and Tom on a previous occasion when I was on a walk with Eliah and Jacob. The walk had "unexpectedly" taken me to the neighborhood Dairy Queen where I decided I had to partake for the good of the local economy. Their nanny Candace, whom I knew and recognized immediately, was with them. She was an international student at Judson, and I had talked with her many times during the last several years. We all sat around the outdoor table, enjoyed our cones, and took time to share and compare our family stories. It was one of those instant camaraderie experiences, as we both laughed at God's hand in our family developments.

An hour later, when the boys and I had returned from the walk, Beth came by our house and dropped off a bunch of girl clothes for Angie, and a friendship quickly blossomed. Several weeks afterward, we learned that Tom was our niece Amie's soccer coach. Time and time again the Lord brought specific people into our lives for the very purpose of ministering to us and through us during this astonishing journey of parenthood.

So kindred friends and mothers were connected on that long-distance call from Angie in California to Beth in Illinois, and it turned out to be extremely helpful. She reminded us that every child is a blessing from the Lord, and that every child is on His schedule, not ours. They laughed and cried and shared mothering stories. It is impossible to talk with Beth for any prolonged period without laughter and joy being involved. It was a well-placed phone call. I needed the vicarious encouragement more than Angie and felt it, though I only listened from a bed over.

As I sat there listening to the schoolgirl enthusiasm they

both projected, I was suddenly struck by the remarkable difference between male and female friendships. When I work out and play hoops with my close buddies, there's always a lot of joshing and kidding each other going on, about everything: our declining strength, speed, athletic skills, and our plans for future achievements. All are topics that have to do with how we're handling the world on our own terms, and we're curious and comparing to see if our friends are doing the same.

But Angie and Beth were NOT checking each other out for recent achievements; they were supporting each other at the deepest possible emotional level. No joshing, no kidding, no roasting, no boasting—pure support with no other purpose than to share, almost join, a friend's emotional circumstances. And by doing that, the acceptance and joy is manifested simultaneously.

At the end of the phone call, despite the benefit we both received, we recommitted not to tell our mothers right away. We knew they would be way too worried, and we didn't want to alarm them just yet. Like us, they were just getting over last year's ordeal.

At the conference the next morning, I found it too difficult to attend any of the sessions or discussion groups. I also wanted to avoid Dr. Simmons because I wasn't sure I could contain myself from telling him the incredible news. Dale obviously noticed my absence and called the room after the second meeting to see if Angie and I wanted to go to lunch. We accepted his invitation and we were able to keep the secret to ourselves. If I would have been alone, I would have caved under the unspoken pressure!

On the flight back to Chicago, we began to have peace and to accept our new and wonderful dilemma. We quietly brainstormed together about extra help around the house and the need to create yet another new daily schedule for our increasing family.

Dale's wife picked us up from the airport and filled us in on all the recent developments within the Judson College campus community. The most interesting, by far, was the shocking news that Tory and Sandy Gum were pregnant again! I about choked on my stick of gum. They had just given birth to their fourth child last year and everyone, including them, I believe, assumed they were done.

In the back of the car, Angie and I exchanged knowing looks as we chuckled internally at the fun we would have telling the Gums that we too were with child again. Tory had been my choice for initial disclosure—this was just going to add to the fun of the announcement!

HERE I AM WITH THE BOYS AT CALVARY BAPTIST CHURCH

CHAPTER 22

Unreleased Anxiety

Without exception, every single person we shared the pregnancy with over the next three months laughed when they heard the shocking declaration. And inevitably, the first words out of their mouth were "Wow! Are you going to have your hands full!" We had told our mothers after much prayer and much vacillating, and both responded wonderfully, despite, I am sure, their inner fears and concerns. They didn't laugh, but they didn't faint, yell, cry, or get angry either. Considering the situation and the near-death experience we had already been through, I would have understood had any of those reactions surfaced. They probably did in private, and our dads probably had to receive them for us.

We also began calling and visiting other mothers of multiples. We specifically sought out their advice and counsel for these early years, and they encouraged us by telling us that even though it would be tough, it would actually reap major benefits once the babies became toddlers. The kids would always have someone to interact with, and they'd never get bored. They were right! Just having an even number of kids has been very helpful to family harmony, for example. But at that point in the equation, the shock did not allow us to look ahead that far.

With bated breath for a healthy pregnancy, we settled into our old routine, but there was yet another wrinkle to iron out. Vicki was in the last trimester of her first pregnancy and now she was experiencing some signs of pre-eclampsia. Not even our baby help could avoid a pregnancy/birthing crisis! Around Thanksgiving time, her doctor ordered her on a program of complete rest. This was at the same juncture that Angie began to experience nausea and fatigue (not that a mother of three infants wasn't going to be tired with or without another baby in the womb). We needed some help again in a big way, and thankfully, the holiday school schedule was conducive for me to flex some hours and take some extended vacation days.

As the end of the semester at Judson approached, we decided to alter our traditional holiday traveling schedule to make it a little less stressful on everybody. Instead of making the trips to Iowa and Cincinnati consecutively, we thought it would be much wiser to space them out in a month's time, but stay longer at each.

With that in mind, we left for Iowa right after the final exam period was over, which was about ten days before Christmas. We stayed there for five days and enjoyed the visit immensely. Bob and Susie were willing and able caretakers of the children while

Angie got some much needed rest. I also was able to rest some and revel in some stretches of quality father time away from my office and home projects. During that time, back in Elgin, Vicki delivered a healthy and beautiful baby girl named Alison. There were now going to be four babies in the house, all of whom were under two years of age with a fifth "on deck."

When we returned to Elgin, the whole family promptly got the flu. All three of the children took turns vomiting for the entire week. Angie stayed remarkably calm despite endless loads of wash, repeated carpet clean-ups, and an infant or three attached to her limbs. She also was able to fight off the virus and was only nauseous for a day or two and threw up only twice. I remained healthy until Christmas Eve, but then got it bad! I spent all of that night and all of Christmas Day in agony and completely useless to Angie for parenting participation for the kids, who were now back to normal.

Early Christmas morning, I called 911 in the form of Angie's parents, and asked if they would be able to come to the rescue — yet again! They obliged, and were at our place by early afternoon, bailing us out of the worst part of the flu storm. For their efforts and sacrifice, after they returned to their home, they both became very ill, as well. That is true love and sacrifice for your children and grandchildren! That is taking one for the team!

Two days later, in order to keep the family traditions alive and not to miss out on the Anderson side of Christmas, we packed up our van and headed to Cincinnati. We had a wonderful time there, as well, and everyone stayed flu free! This holiday season's altered schedules, illness, and nanny adjustments were not the only changes that began to bog down our well-oiled baby care machine.

Our first hint that things would be greatly different during this pregnancy occurred when we learned that the obstetrics office that had handled the care of Angie and the delivery of Alivia closed just months after she was born. This was not a surprise. Our midwife had warned us of this business decision early on in our association with them.

What we did not expect, however, were the nightmare insurance-coverage problems. Angie spent over a year battling and hassling with the insurance companies to process all of our bills. Her records were supposedly not moved or stored properly, and to this day we don't know where they all are. More importantly, however, was that the midwife and the doctors who had saved Angie and Alivia from catastrophe were no longer available to us. This bothered me physically and emotionally.

Our second major cog was when Vicki contracted an infection and had a difficult time in rebounding. On doctor's orders, she had to take some more time off from hands-on love and care of our three children. Angie also started to slow down as she neared the second trimester and began to experience the first noticeable decrease in her stamina. My schedule at work had been ideal over the holidays, but now I was back to regular long hours and had to deal with several student discipline problems as soon as the second semester was underway.

Once again we had to rely on friends, family, and our two support communities at that time (Judson College and Calvary Baptist Church) to help us get through the month. Several ladies at the church and many of my peers at Judson offered help and brought food to feed both our family and Vicki's. By the end of January, Vicki's health stabilized and she was able to return to her normal hours and was helped by the fact that Alison began to sleep for some extended periods during the night. It was a long, hard, difficult two months, but without our loved ones it could have been potentially devastating!

Our primary care physician, Dr. Soctt Varley, alleviated one of these major issues when he advised us to see his colleague, a high-risk specialist obstetrician in Elgin, Dr. William Mattviuw. We scheduled an appointment and put ourselves in his hands for the entire pregnancy and delivery. At every visit, he assured us that Angie showed no unusual signs and that the baby was strong and healthy. The more time we spent with Dr. Mattviuw, the more we liked him and the more we trusted his opinion.

Despite his excellent care and the relative ease of the second pregnancy, it was I, not Angie, who started to express and display high levels of anxiety. At first, I dismissed my strange thoughts as just normal fatherly overprotection. I had noticed it creep into my conscious behavior over the last year and a half. Soon, though, my fears became too obsessive and too disturbing to remove from my mind, and they spilled out into my reality. I was absolutely sure that one of the children was going to drown or get fatally hurt, and nothing Angie would say or do would convince me otherwise.

The primary manifestation of this fear would come in the form of nagging Angie at meal times. I would watch her cut up the fruit and vegetables for the children and nearly jump out of my skin. She used an ordinary kitchen knife in an ordinary way, but I was convinced she would bump her elbow or stumble over a high chair and accidentally cut one of the children with the knife.

To put this anxiety expression into a more complete context, you must realize that this kind of reactionary response is 100% contrary to my normal existence. That is what made it all the more difficult for Angie to process. She tried to answer my irrational questions and did her best to submit to my ridiculous requests, but it was hard for her to understand how I could go from one extreme to the other. Nevertheless, my fears escalated until I was convinced that Angie or the unborn baby or both were going to perish during delivery, and a fatalistic doom engulfed me.

Finally, after pleadings from my wife and on the suggestion from my friend and colleague, LeAnn Pauley Heard, the Dean of Students, I scheduled an appointment with her husband, Dr. Warren Heard. Dr. Heard had been my favorite seminary professor at Trinity, and then he had come to Judson to teach. It didn't take long for Dr. Heard to understand my problem, and we discussed ways to help me process this reality. Here was his quick assessment and analysis of my unordinary, for me at least, anxiety.

What had happened was that I had not fully emotionalized and processed the horrific events of the near-death of both Angie and Alivia during that frightening C-section delivery—with all the memories of blood, drugs, tubes, clamps, scalpels, and doctors and nurses rushing helter skelter to keep the most important person in my world, and our unborn child, alive.

Because things had worked out so well and because there was never any spare time to pause and reflect upon the whole traumatic event, the emotions had been unreleased and were beginning to interfere with my reality. Even though I am an experienced psychologist and counselor, the need in my soul to heal from those wounds was the same as it would have been for anyone else. And now that I was in the mental and emotional stages of another birthing experience, that lack of closure and the need for grieving was re-ignited. His prescription strategy was simple. He encouraged me to try and express to Angie how terrified I had really been during the whole whirlwind crisis and to do so soon.

I can't recall if it was that same night or several nights later, but I do recall that once I reached into my psyche and began to tell her how scared I really had been that morning, the emotional dam broke loose and the floodgates opened profusely. I sobbed uncontrollably for fifteen minutes and then struggled for another fifteen minutes to regain my composure. I verbalized all of the fears that had raced through my mind as she lay there barely conscious while the doctors hurried to save the suffocating baby. I confessed my concern that if she and Alivia had died I would have had to raise two nine-month-old baby boys by myself, a widower. Our children are not the only ones who depend on Angie's organization, structure, and scheduled lifestyle and personality!

Angie held me and accepted my fears and concerns because they were not being expressed in an anxious, overprotective, hostile style. This time the concerns were being shared from the depths of my soul. I wondered if Angie knew that some of these kinds of feelings had been trapped because she did not seem too surprised or moved by my cathartic collapse. She probably had enough of her own anxiety brewing, but could not begin to release it until I was emotionally healthy again.

After gaining control of my emotions, I explained the other relevant things that Dr. Heard had suggested to me. My current anxiety was so intense and uncontrollable because now that she was pregnant again, and with the high-risk status, with or without three other babies at home, my deep unconscious was triggering itself to automatically associate this second pregnancy with the previous life-or-death trauma.

The next morning I felt better, but it was not overnight, instant relief. I still dealt with some floating anxiety the rest of the pregnancy, but the intensity and the frequency of the attacks definitely subsided. Another way that I worked through the fears was to admit them to my family and friends. I had often been the one they had talked to when they had been through similar life ordeals, so the reciprocal approach was received well.

One of the more effective therapeutic tools I use as a counselor is to teach my students about self-disclosure, vulnerability, and the need to lean on trusted love ones during times of emotional trouble. I found out, again, firsthand, how truly important this biblical principle is to mental health.

PAIGE IS GETTING READY FOR A NAP

Chapter 23

Another Paige in the Story

Early in March of 2002, we found out the new baby was a girl and would arrive in July. Angie wanted to know the sex because, in her words, "I can't take any more surprises in my life right now." This child was clearly bigger than Alivia had ever been. We could see signs of the baby kicking and stretching on the skin surface of Angie's tummy, especially at night. She was so active and so busy we assumed we had another "live wire" on our hands. This time we settled on the name Paige well ahead of the due date. I had a good friend throughout my childhood named Paige and had always liked the name. Angie liked it as well, and we added her maternal grandmother's name of Katherine as her middle name. It felt good to have something solidified prematurely, just in case there was more chaos and craziness on the horizon.

In May we got the great news that Julie Schilling, my sister's college roommate from Judson in the 90s, had decided to come back to Elgin for the summer. She was a third grade teacher in

Michigan and wanted to get out of the house for the summer. She volunteered to help out with the children in return for room and board and the fun of "hanging out" with old friends again!

This was another unsolicited gargantuan blessing for us, one we had not thought of, prayed for, or even contemplated! Julie is an experienced elementary school teacher, and she would be moving in with us from mid-June to mid-August! Praise the Lord for friends who followed God's promptings in their life to jump in and join the ride with us!

By late June, Angie was getting a little uncomfortable, but not showing any indication of pre-eclampsia. Dr. Mattviuw continued to be pleased with the baby's development, and he noted that the child was unusually long. By early July we were surprised that Angie had no sensations of delivery approaching and no feeling whatsoever that the baby was getting into position for birth.

As much as we had been mentally prepared for something else to happen, we couldn't believe we were facing another "extreme" in our parenting lives. From infertility, to adoption, to failed adoption, to successful adoption, to a dangerous premature birth, and now—to an overdue baby!

Finally, on Monday, July 9th, a couple of days past the latest guess of a due date, at our already scheduled appointment, Dr. Mattviuw began to discuss options for what we might want or need to do. Paige was still doing very well, but the doctor was getting concerned because Angie is a small-framed woman, has a narrow birth canal, and was still not showing signs of delivery. She had not dilated at all, and her cervix was not ripening. All along, Angie had wanted to have a vaginal birth, but if complications were to arise, she was quite willing do what Dr. Mattviuw might suggest. And that time of danger was getting close. Finally, near the end of the examination, Dr. Mattviuw advised us to schedule a C-section.

Tears welled up in Angie's eyes, and she quietly expressed her sadness in the notion that she would once again not be able to experience a "normal" delivery. Dr. Mattviuw was most considerate and gentle, but explained that vaginal birth in her current bodily state would probably entail a 24-to-36-hour period of labor, with the likely result being another C-section anyway. Why bother with all that misery when she could show up at the hospital rested and ready to go through the whole preparation and delivery in just a couple of hours?

This description of the options, coupled with our trust in Dr. Mattviuw's expertise, and the memories of Alivia's high-octane birth, made the decision rather easy. We called his office the next day, and scheduled a C-section for Friday, July 12, at 7:00 AM.

This scheduled delivery also made it much easier for our families and close friends to plan their shifts for helping and visits. Both sets of parents timed their next trip for that weekend, and Julie and Vicki made all the necessary adjustments to take care of the three siblings plus Alison at home—Eliah and Jacob, who had just turned two, and Alivia, who was fifteen months.

The scheduled C-section also gave me peace of mind. We had been through one before and this time would do so without all the fears generated by the state of emergency! We had a nice time of prayer the night before, and both of us slept well. Ready or not, it was time to bring another baby into the world and time to bring another child into our family. WOW! When was this roller coaster going to dock for a while? I was beginning to get woozy from the adrenaline rushes!

On Friday morning we woke up early, showered and packed, and slipped out of the house before any of the older children had awakened. We arrived at the hospital about 6:05 AM and filled out all the paperwork. The staff did some basic check-up procedures on Angie while we waited for Dr. Mattviuw to arrive. We talked, and prayed, and asked many questions of the other doctors and staff, checking to see how different a scheduled C-section might be from an emergency one.

There were, in fact, many differences. The most important was recovery. Without the life-or-death scenario, the doctor could take his time and would not need to cut through Angie's stomach muscles to get to the birthing sac. He could be more deliberate and particular about how he approached the baby. And without all the drugs and the time needed to heal the muscles, Angie would recover twice as quickly. With three little ones at home, this was a very important bonus.

Around 7:00 AM Nurse Weber came to spend the morning with us. In one of those mysterious feminine relational differences, Angie and Susan cried together as they discussed the surgery. Seventy men could have entered the room, and Angie would not have cried (except, perhaps, if her father had entered), but the tears began immediately when Susan came through the door. I was right there with her from start to finish and we had not cried together. I wasn't jealous, but the intimacy differences were very interesting!

At 8:00 AM Dr. Mattviuw arrived as positive as ever, and explained the details of the surgery and the timetable for the rest of the day. His confidence was soothing, and we really did trust him. His reputation had been earned by years of success in just such circumstances.

At 9:00 AM the nurses wheeled Angie's bed down to the operating room while I waited in the hallway as she was prepped further and strapped down. When I was allowed in the room, there were seven or eight people at work. Angie's abdomen was revealed, and it was the focus of everyone's attention. This time, I could turn on my observational antennae and really survey the environment.

The room was cold and metallic and everything was white. It had a heavenly aura to it. The staff bustled around but not in the frenetic manner of the emergency Cesarean. Many of the doctors and nurses appeared to be smiling, though I couldn't know for sure with their masks on. I assumed they either had heard about our story or were just joyful for their role in bringing life into being. The whole atmosphere was much less frightening and much calmer than before. I took a deep breath and headed for my support role with dignity.

Only Dr. Mattviuw and the head nurse were talking, giving barely audible directives to the staff. It was obvious to me that he was in charge and in control and that he did not appreciate mindless or useless chatter in his operation room. Like before, the air was full of lots of little bleeps, squeaks, and other assorted noises, but this time, they weren't startling; they were comforting.

After several minutes of busyness, Dr. Mattviuw popped his head up over the screen that prevented us from watching the actual operation. He nodded his head to his staff and said, "Shall we begin?" It was like a Doc-in-the-box without the music.

First, a nurse gave Angie a local anesthetic to numb her from the waist down. Then Dr. Mattviuw made a major incision right on top of the scar from the first C-section. We know this because he was giving us a play by play! He explained to us that he was taking a little extra time here to make some aesthetic improvements on the area that the previous doctors didn't have time to work on because of the emergency conditions. This again was another bonus we had not thought to ask for or anticipated.

Then his assistants clamped both sides of Angie's abdominal

wall muscles so that he could bring the birthing sac out without tearing any muscle fibers. Just like in the first C-section, this act of throwing the birthing sac up on to Angie's rib cage caused her whole body to give one big spasm from the shock, the weight, and the sudden impact. A minute or two later we could hear the baby rustling as the doctor's machines sucked up the surrounding fluids and presto, over the screen a tiny baby girl appeared.

Even in that fresh-from-the-womb state, a baby is a very special sight to behold. She was beautiful! But to our complete surprise, she had dark hair and darker skin than Alivia. Because Alivia was so fair all the way around, and because Angie and I had been "tow heads" as children, the dark features were really unexpected.

One of the nurses asked if I wanted to cut the umbilical cord. I politely declined. Another nurse asked if I wanted to go over to the warming table and watch the initial tests and clean-up procedures. Again, I politely declined. I wanted to stay with Angie until the nurses completed their procedures with her. Angie was obviously pleased with my decision because she gave me a loving glance and squeeze of the hand.

Within a few minutes Angie was sewn up and able to return to her room. While she was recuperating I was again the fortunate one who got to spend the time with my newborn daughter during the first few minutes of her life. She was indeed a long baby at 22 inches, but she was not particularly heavy for her length, just 7 pounds 9 ounces.

Her face was also broader than Alivia's, though she had the same big, bright, blue eyes. I did end up getting to watch her go through several of the first tests, and she passed them all with flying colors. The nurse said it would be a couple of hours before I could take her in to see her mother, so I left her with the nurses for a while and went back to join Angie and give her an update on her second daughter and her fourth child, all two years of age and under!

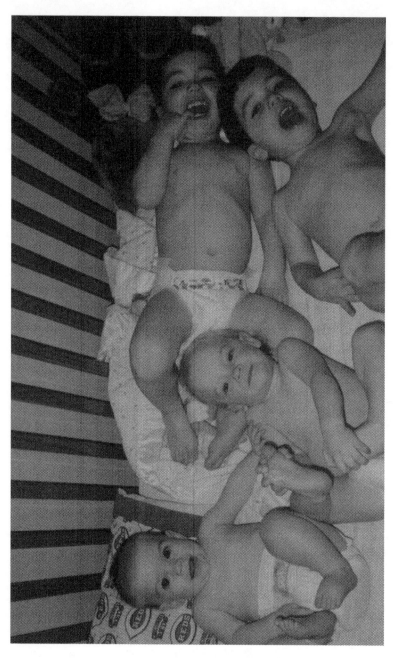

OUR BOUNTY OF BLESSINGS

CHAPTER 24

Answers in Abundance

Our immediate family was once again waiting for us when we returned home from the hospital with Paige. Yet another celebration ensued, though they were getting less dramatic each time around. It was July 14, 2002. From the day we went to Wheaton to pick up the boys till the day we came home with Paige was exactly two years and fifteen days! After all those years of waiting and yearning, the Lord answered our prayers in abundance by bringing four children into our home in two years! It was an amazing journey. It was an enormously challenging start to parenting!

With the addition of a fourth came another round of adjustments and needs. An additional timing issue was that with Alivia's March arrival we had had the whole summer to adjust before the college was in session. Paige's July arrival left us only one month to prepare. I feared a difficult transition period of sleep-deprived nights and I was right.

Another Anderson who had a tough transition was Alivia.

Alivia was Mama's girl from the minute she got home from the hospital. Since the boys had always been Daddy's boys, this fit nicely into the family system. Now, however, Alivia had to share Mom, and she was not at all happy about it. Angie used to always be the one to lay Alivia down for the night—now she wanted Dad. Alivia used to cuddle with Mom when the family watched a video —now she wanted to cuddle with Dad. Bath time, feeding time, reading time, comfort time—now all Dad, Dad, Dad, Dad.

All of this shifting would have been fine if she had been the only other sibling in the house. Eliah and Jacob, though, were not very excited about sharing their Dad time with her anymore than they already had to due to their twin factor. This necessary sharing of parental attention initiated the intense sibling rivalries that we knew would exist when they were older, but that surprised us by this early onset. This also coincided with the development and expression of Alivia's personality, which displayed a fiery competitive nature, just like mine.

Paige, thank the Lord, was a very complacent baby. She did not react negatively to minor adjustments in her routine, and Angie took advantage of her demeanor to alleviate some of the frustrations of her siblings. The household ended up divided into two camps for the first three months of Paige's life. Vicki and I and the four older children (Eliah, Jacob, Alivia, and Alison) were one subset and Angie and Paige were the other.

I know this may sound selfish and typical of males, but the

single hardest aspect of the shift in life was that the other passions of my life were essentially on hold or nonexistent for three years. I went from drumming weekly to annually. I can count the times I played competitive basketball from 2000 – 2003 on one hand. My yearly reading program went from an average of forty books to five. Even this writing project suffered. It had already downshifted after Alivia was born, but then it went into a grinding neutral after Paige arrived. Don't misunderstand my reporting of this reality. I wouldn't trade the experiences or the results for anything, but the extreme nature of our childrearing explosion was certainly taxing.

Angie, too, had to forgo her side interests and hobbies. Her shopping trips became based on necessity and convenience rather than pleasure and strategy. Her antiquing went into hibernation and has not yet wakened. Her gardening and lawn work was buried for five years. Her cooking and baking was solely for life preservation for a season. And she never got to leave the home for work five days a week for an eight-to-nine-hour separation period! I don't know how she did it other than the Lord equips us with exactly what we need to handle the things that He gives us.

It was during one of those weeks of extreme fatigue in the early fall of 2002 that I told Angie we were going to have to get more help. My emotional reserve felt completely depleted, and we weren't even in October. I couldn't fathom the long winter months with no outdoor play opportunities and without additional hands. We began to ask family and friends for contacts to see if anyone knew a female with some childcare experience who would want to trade room and board for some part time nanny duties. It was only a short time later that our friend Linda Schnabel called Angie with a possible match.

Kara Piazza came over on a Saturday afternoon in October to meet Angie and be introduced to the children for basically an informal interview. Although she was very quiet and reserved, the kids loved her immediately, and she was engaged in their activities within minutes of her arrival. Kara was a youth pastor at a suburban church and was dating a Judson alum that Angie and I had known for some time. She lived in Aurora, about a half hour south of Elgin, and was interested in moving toward our area. We cleared out the spare bedroom on the second floor and in November Kara moved in. I don't know if I would have mentally survived the winter without her.

Kara and Angie agreed on a schedule of Monday, Wednesday, and Friday afternoons from 4:00 – 8:00 PM and some selected Saturdays and Sundays for special needs or events. Kara quickly assimilated to our routines and structure and was proactive and assertive in addressing obvious needs of the clan. She soon became Paige's personal attendant, teaching her how to walk and taking her on special one-on-one trips. Paige absolutely loved the extra attention. Sometime around Christmas, and in yet another moment of startling providential revelation and confirmation of

God's hand upon our parenting journey, we found out that Kara and Paige shared the same birthday!

We also received some additional unexpected and unsolicited help from our church. On Tuesday and Thursday afternoons, Tigan Gelinas, a high school student, came over for roughly the same late afternoon to early evening timeframe. She had been helping out somewhat regularly since Alivia had been born and was already accepted as extended family. She wouldn't accept money from us, so we gave her respite from her home and an assortment of free Judson gear.

This need for such regular around-the-clock assistance is very humbling. You know your emotions are vulnerable when your mood will plummet if you find out your high school helper can't make it for the day! This state of dependence on others, though, is a healthy creator of relational community. In a nutshell, that is probably what the process of adoption and the miraculous, but extreme biological-parenting experience taught us the most. Community is a Biblical mandate and an obvious benefit to all involved. Our children have about fifteen adults that they have significantly bonded with and have received enormous amounts of love and attention from our caring friends.

Even when we stopped needing the help, which was around the summer of 2004, we continued to have college girls live with us in exchange for a date night for Angie and me so we could invest in the marriage separate from the children. Besides Kara, we had Erin Rasor, Laura Kovacik (two different times), and Andrea Dukey take part in Family Anderson. I hope we blessed them as much as they blessed us.

The single most personal movement of the answers in abundance, however, was not from the answers that the Lord gave us. No, it was the answer that I finally gave Him!

THE FULFILLMENT OF THE ANSWERS

CHAPTER 25

Answering the Call

Sometime during the grieving and healing process of the adoption, my heart and soul returned to previously buried promptings and leadings to become a pastor. I finally said "Yes" to God's call on my life. Ever since college, I had wrestled with whether or not I had a call or just an interest, but deep within my soul I think I always knew. The parenting journey just brought it to the surface.

I believe that this is often the way the Lord speaks to us. He capitalizes on our broken state, when we are desperate and dependent on Him and more apt to listen, and consequently, to follow!

So, in the midst of all the rest of our chaos, I scheduled a breakfast with Pastor Tim and told him what I thought the Lord was telling me. It felt good to get it out in the open and off my chest, but then he didn't do anything about it! Pastor Tim did not seem too surprised by my disclosure, and he encouraged me to continue to pray about it and seek the Lord's guidance, but he did nothing else as far as mentoring or counseling. No follow-up of any kind! No email, no phone call, no conversation in the church foyer, nothing!

I didn't take it personally, but I was a bit confused. Pastor Tim is extremely good with people and super fun to be around, and I had spent some significant time with his son, so I thought if nothing else, he owed me some coaching in this process. After two months of silence, I called him again and we went out to eat again. I reiterated the call on my heart and asked him how I should begin to move forward in this endeavor.

He recommended that I start by getting licensed so that I could get my feet wet before doing something drastic with my well-founded career at Judson. He said we should not rush into ministry in the midst of all the other changes Angie and I were already experiencing. I agreed with that wisdom and told him I had no intention of leaving Judson; I was just being obedient to what I knew God wanted me to do. He said he would talk to the deacon board and get back to me. Two more months later—I had heard nothing.

This time I was a little irritated, but too busy to invest any energy in silly feelings, so I simply called him again and scheduled another breakfast! This time he told me the whole truth. He had been sitting on my call because he knew my personality, knew my current family situation, and knew my commitment to Judson. He was not about to do something flippant and random just to satisfy my curiosity. He had to make sure that my heart was completely sold out and 100% sincere. My continued perseverance in moving forward after six months was what he needed to see. He had peace about it now and would talk to the deacons immediately. I was relieved and grateful for his wisdom and testing. That time of contemplation was helpful to me as well, as I knew I could not back down or suppress the call any longer.

True to his word, a meeting with the deacon board was scheduled for the next Tuesday evening. I was to come by myself and to simply explain to the deacons what God had placed on my heart. This was not a difficult thing to do for a talker like me, but it was even easier, because half of the board consisted of Judson alumni—and two of them were my former basketball teammates!

We decided at that meeting to go through an evaluative period while working toward a ministerial license. Because I was already so loaded with teaching/counseling duties and experience, they simply required me to keep a log of my work, which would now include some substitute teaching for Sunday school and also for Sunday evening pulpit supply at Calvary.

About four months later, I met with the board again for a review. This meeting also included a question and answer time for Angie. Before we were to go in front of the whole congregation, they wanted to make sure that Angie was completely behind the call and whatever would come from it. Of course she was, and we both communicated our willingness to go where God orchestrated, though neither of us expected the speed at which God was about to work. After all of God's workings in the "just add water" family of six we now had, how could we be so naïve?

In January of 2004, Angie and I stood before the congregation of Calvary Baptist Church to reveal God's call on our life. Pastor Tim explained the process that had been already in place and presented me with my ministerial license. We shared with the Body that we knew that I would be a pastor at a church sometime in the future. I made this specific statement that once again proved to be providential: "It might be in six months or it might be in twenty years, but I know this call to pastor is for real, and we will follow His lead."

The Lord must have been tuned in and just waiting for that kind of profession and confession from me, for six months later, in July of 2004, I was a candidate for the senior pastor position at Elgin Evangelical Free Church! And, isn't God amazing, for they answered "Yes" also!

BROCK AND VANESSA HENDERSON

FAMILY AT BROCK AND VANESSA'S WEDDING, FALL 2005

EPILOGUE

It has been almost seven years now since I decided to put our names on the list to attend the introductory meeting at Sunny Ridge Family Center to learn about becoming adoptive parents. I consider it the third-best decision I have ever made. The first is when I asked Jesus Christ to be my Lord and Savior and when I turned my stubborn and rebellious will over to the Holy Spirit midway through my sophomore year at college. The second is when I asked Angie to be my wife and allowed myself, over time, to be truly intimate and vulnerable with my partner and experience the incredible blessing of a united, one-flesh relationship.

The third, as I mentioned, is the decision to begin our parenting journey through the adoption option. Although this book has been the story of our entire parenting journey, the decision to adopt and the ensuing process has been nothing short of a divine anointing—a true miracle.

One of the most frequent questions friends ask us is if, in hindsight, we would have still gone through the adoption process if we would have known we were going to eventually be able to conceive and have children biologically. Though I completely understand the question and am not offended by it, the question has no relevance for us. Let me explain why.

If the adoption process and Eliah and Jacob had not been a part of our family and our experience as parents, then the family as we know it would not exist. To us, it is the same as asking someone who has not adopted, but has four biological children, whether they would have had the first two children if they would have known that they were going to give birth to two more! Of course they would have!

The first two children were born first and were the beginning of their family. The second two were born later and were the ending of their family. The order of the family and how it developed is as important as the total number of children.

Furthermore, you must consider the uniqueness and the timing of each birth and the resulting individual personalities of the children and how they are affected by their siblings and the birth order. The exact same is true of our scenario. Take Eliah and Jacob out of our family as the first born sons and there is no family as we know it. It is almost the equivalent of imagining my life without Christ in it. Everything would be different and every decision and choice would be made from a different perspective. There is no point in second-guessing or living in hindsight.

In fact, going through the adoption process has deepened and strengthened my relationship with Christ and my understanding of some important theological concepts. For example, I have never understood my relationship with Jesus Christ as an adopted son of God better than I have now that I am an adoptive father. There is absolutely NO difference in my love, attention, dreams, discipline, nurturance, affection, frustration, and joy that I receive and give to Eliah and Jacob in comparison to the same with Alivia and Paige. Just like Christ has no difference in his love for any of his children—all ethnicities, all ages, and all levels of functioning. All four of our children are gifts from God and all four are equal heirs in the Kingdom of God and equal heirs in the family of Anderson.

The president of Judson College, Dr. Jerry Cain, calls Angie and me the poster couple for "adoptive families," and in a wonderful way, we have become a resource and answer center for alumni and friends in our community regarding fertility issues and adoption. It is a position we hold with great honor and responsibility, as we attempt to advocate for adoption as an option, without pressuring or pushing couples to feel shame or guilt if they are not comfortable moving or thinking in that direction.

Three times already in my career as a pastor, on mornings I mentioned something about our infertility experience, there just happened to be couples visiting who had been suffering in silence for years! Coincidence? Of course not! It is just the hand of God continuing to use our experience to help others on their journey.

All three couples have joined the church and one of those couples is now in the adoption process themselves.

Again, it is very similar to evangelism. You can preach and teach and share about the love of Jesus, but you can't force someone into choosing to accept Christ as his or her Savior. It still comes down to a revelation from the Holy Spirit and the individual decision of each person to act upon that conviction and leading.

Adoption is not the automatic best answer for everybody! But it was definitely the right answer for us and the obedient answer for us, and God has blessed us and many others through this story. Praise God from whom all blessing flow! Praise God for His answers in abundance!

ELGIN  EVANGELICAL FREE CHURCH

The Elgin Evangelical Free Church has been a committed body of believers proclaiming the gospel of Jesus Christ for over 110 years! It is a member of the Evangelical Free Church of America (EFCA) which is an association of 1,100 autonomous churches joined together by common purposes, principles, and practices. The Free Church also includes a worldwide ministry of 600 churches and 11 mission fields. The EFCA has established a reputation throughout the world for soundness of biblical doctrine, Christian fellowship, emphasis on holy living and freedom to embrace Christian people from all walks of life.

The mission of the Elgin Evangelical Free Church to impact our world for Jesus Christ by loving God, loving people, and making disciples. Our mission and our logo our based on the teachings of Jesus found in the Great Commandment and the Great Commission.

To learn more about the Elgin Evangelical Free Church visit us online at **www.elginefc.org** or call us at **(847) 695-8812**.

Sunday School	9:15 AM
Morning Worship Service	10:30 AM
Evening Service	6:00 PM

JUDSON UNIVERSITY

Consistently ranked in the top tier of U.S. News & World Report's "America's Best Colleges," Judson University is a four-year Christian university of the liberal arts, sciences and professions, committed to an evangelical expression of Christian faith and living.

Judson offers four-year BA programs with more than 60 majors, minors and concentrations to choose from. Judson also offers an accelerated BA program for adult students and graduate programs in Architecture, Education and Organizational Leadership. The university has campuses in Elgin and Rockford, IL and a student body of approximately 1,200.

Recently, Judson put itself "on the map" with the construction of an innovative "green" academic center to house the university's library and rapidly growing division of art, design and architecture. The academic center is expected to be one of the most energy efficient buildings of its kind in North America.

For more information, visit our website at

www.judsoncollege.edu or call **847 628-1498**

Sunny Ridge Family Center
www.sunnyridge.org

Sunny Ridge Family Center—a licensed, faith-based, non-profit agency, invites you to consider adoption with the help of our agency. Come learn about children available from the United States, as well as China, Guatemala, Ethiopia, Poland, the Philippines and more. Learn the requirements and process for adopting.

Our Mission: Serving children and building families around the world.

Have you recently considered adoption?

Not sure where to start?

For more information, visit our website at **www.sunnyridge.org** or call **(800) 222-9666**.

encourage equip connect deliver
www.AriseCorp.org

ARISE! has spent years working with Native American leaders and their communities. More importantly, we have listened to the cry of their hearts for the restoration of hope in their peoples lives. The Arise model offers you or your organization a wonderful multi-level opportunity to engage in cross-cultural missions outreaches within North America. We can help you form a meaningful relationship with godly Native American Christian leaders, their communities and people. We offer training to help you understand and embrace the vast culture and traditions of the Native American people. We strive for long-term relationships and to that end we shepherd and nurture through each phase of our model. The result for your organization can be heart-felt racial reconciliation and the birth of a cross-cultural mission outreach opportunity that is close to home. In this way ARISE! Ministries is a blessing to both the native and non-native church!

If you are interested in a long or short-term missions trip with your church, organization, or ministry, we invite you to contact us at **AriseCorp@gmail.com** so we may pray through what the Lord has for you in this forgotten treasure.

Paper Tower, founded by Brock Henderson—Elliott's brother-in-law, is a innovative design studio located in Elgin, Illinois. We help businesses and organizations stand out from the crowd by partnering with clients and journeying through the creative process together. We bring to the table a team with a broad range of skills and expertise, a passion for design, and a sense of humor.

We help clients of all sizes create dynamic, memorable experiences that are consistent across multiple mediums and that remain on target with the their vision and budget. With services in branding, web design, graphic design, motion graphics, video editing and compositing, animation, package design, and game design—we can help you create a solution no matter what your design need.

To learn more about how Paper Tower can help your business or organization, visit us online at **www.papertower.com** or give us a call at **847-513-2063**.

9 781600 372322